Link ◀▶ Word

FRENCH
by Association

Dr. Michael M. Gruneberg

PASSPORT BOOKS

NTC/Contemporary Publishing Company

ISBN: 0-8442-9445-4

Published by Passport Books,
a division of NTC/Contemporary Publishing Company,
4255 West Touhy Avenue,
Lincolnwood (Chicago), Illinois 60646-1975 U.S.A.

7 8 9 0 VP 9 8 7 6 5 4 3 2

CONTENTS

SECTION 7

SECTION 8

SECTION 9

SECTION 10

FOREWORD

Anyone reading a book that teaches a foreign language might well wonder why it has been written by a memory expert and not a linguist or a language teacher. Well, the simple fact is that if you want to *remember* what you are taught, then putting ease of remembering at the center of the design of the book is likely to lead to far higher levels of learning than a book written only with the ideas of a linguist in mind. Of course, this book has been written by a memory expert working with skilled linguists so that the language aspects are correct.

The basic "memory idea" of the book to help you remember what you are taught is the "method of association," or the linkword method. Learning a foreign language is all about associating what you are familiar with, e.g., the word *bread,* with something you are not familiar with— the word for *bread* is *pan* in Spanish or Japanese. There are two possible ways you can do this. You can repeat the words *bread* and *pan* together until you are sure it sticks, or you can "picture" yourself putting some bread into a pan. This picturing technique is known as the method of association, or the linkword method. Of course, as far as learning foreign language vocabulary is concerned, there is a further complication that the foreign word may not sound like *any* English word. For example, the Spanish for cow is *vaca,* which sounds like "vaka." What you do in this situation is to imagine a *cow* with a *vacuum* cleaner, cleaning a field. The linkword *vacuum* does not have to be identical to the foreign word in order to be able to associate *cow* with "vaka" through the use of mental pictures. It may sound bizarre, but over fifty studies published in scientific journals have found this technique to materially increase the level of foreign vocabulary learning. In one study of Spanish, for example, learning increased from 28% for rote learning to 88% using the picture association technique.

The method of association was known to the Greeks as an efficient way of improving memory, and the application of the method of association to learning foreign languages was discussed as long ago as the nineteenth century. It is only recently, however, that psychologists have shown how effective the method is when applied to learning foreign language vocabulary, and the present book is, as far as the author is aware, the first to make use of the method to provide a whole course for foreign language learners, teaching not only an extensive vocabulary but providing a basic grammar and using sentence examples.

The course consists of hundreds of useful words that, with the grammar provided, can be strung together to form sentences. In eight to twelve hours, you should be able to go right through the course and acquire enough useful knowledge to communicate when you go abroad.

The author has published a number of studies* of the courses that show how fast and easy people find it. In one study of travel executives, the group was taught Spanish for *twelve* contact hours. They were then tested by an independent test expert who found they were virtually errorless on the four hundred word vocabulary and grammar they had been taught. The independent expert estimated they would normally have taken *forty* hours to reach that standard. In a second study, a group of bankers was taught a vocabulary of at least six hundred words and basic grammar in four days. However, it is not just the linguistically able who benefit from the courses. In one study, thirteen-year-old low-ability language students were given one session every week using the Spanish by Association course and another session using conventional teaching methods for one term. At the end of the term, the students were given a test where the mean vocabulary score on Spanish following conventional teaching was 23.75% compared to 69% for the Spanish by Association course. One student out of sixteen passed with conventional teaching, fourteen out of sixteen passed with the Spanish by Association teaching. The studies carried out to date show that the courses are ideal for anyone who wants to learn the basics of a language in a hurry, whether for travel, for business, or for schoolwork. For many people such as the tourist who just wants to get by or the business person who has to be in Berlin next Wednesday, then Paris next Friday, their language needs do not involve the mastery of a single language in depth but the rapid acquisition of a basic language to get by with. Because they are designed specifically to enhance speed and ease of language acquisition and to help

*M. M. Gruneberg and G. C. Jacobs (1991), "In Defence of Linkword," *The Language Learning Journal* (3), 25–29.

you remember what you have learned, the By Association courses are uniquely suited to meet such needs, as well as the needs of those who might have experienced language learning difficulties earlier in life.

INTRODUCTION

WHO IS *FRENCH BY ASSOCIATION* FOR?

The short answer is that By Association books are for anyone and
everyone who wants to learn the basics of a language in a hurry. It can be
used by children or by adults. Even young children who cannot read can
be taught French words by a parent reading out the images.

The By Association courses have been carefully designed to teach you
a basic grammar and words in a simple step-by-step way that anyone can
follow. After about ten to twelve hours, or even less, you will have a
vocabulary of literally hundreds of words and the ability to string these
words together to form sentences. The course is ideal, therefore, for the
tourist or business person who just wants the basics in a hurry so he or
she can be understood, e.g., in the hotel, arriving at the destination,
sightseeing, eating out, in emergencies, telling time, and so on.

The course is also an ideal supplement to schoolwork. Many students feel
that they remember words for the first time when introduced to the By
Association system, and understand basic grammar for the first time too!

HOW TO USE *FRENCH BY ASSOCIATION*

1. You will be presented with words like this:
   The French for **tablecloth** is **nappe.**
   Imagine having a **nap** on a **tablecloth.**
   What you do is to imagine this picture in your mind's eye as vividly as possible.

2. After you have read the image for a word, visualize it in your mind's eye for about ten seconds before moving on to the next word. If you do not spend enough time thinking about the image, it will not stick in your memory as well as it should.

3. Sometimes the word in French and in English is the same or very similar. For example, the word for **taxi** in French is **taxi.** When this happens, you will be asked to associate the word in some way with the Eiffel Tower.

   Imagine a taxi driving under the Eiffel Tower. Whenever the Eiffel Tower comes to mind, therefore, you will know the word is the same or similar in English and French.

4. The examples given in the course may well strike you as silly and bizarre. They have deliberately been designed in this way to illustrate points of grammar and to get away from the idea that you should remember useful phrases "parrot fashion."

5. **Accents**
   Accents are given for French words. You may not want to focus so much on remembering accents as on remembering words.

6. Pronunciation

The approximate pronunciation of words is given in parentheses after the word is presented for the first time.

For example: The French for **cabbage** is **chou** (SHOO)
(SHOO) is the way the word is pronounced.

When the following letters appear in the words in parentheses (pronunciation words), they sound like this.

J sounds like the *s* in plea*s*ure.
oo is a rather strange sound—but you will be understood if you pronounce it like the *oo* in l*oo*p.
n sounds like the *N* in fia*n*cé.
e sounds like the *U* in c*u*rl.

Here are some examples:

The French for **garage** is **garage** (GARAJ).
The French for **skirt** is **jupe** (JooP).
The French for **rabbit** is **lapin** (LAPAHn).
The French for **the** is **le** (Le).

Do not worry too much about these pronunciations to begin with. The approximate pronunciation given in parentheses will allow you to be understood.

SOME USEFUL HINTS

1. It is usually best to go through the course as quickly as possible. Many people can get through most of the course in a weekend, especially if they start on Friday evening.

2. Take a break of about ten minutes between each section, and always *stop* if you feel tired.

3. Don't worry about forgetting a few words, and do not go back to relearn words you have forgotten. Just think of how much you are learning, and try to pick up the forgotten words when it comes to reviewing.

4. Review after Section 4, Section 8 and at the end of the course. Then review the whole course a week later and a month later.

5. Don't worry if you forget some of the words or grammar after a time. Relearning is extremely fast, and going through the book for a few hours just before you go abroad will quickly get you back to where you were.

6. The course will not give you conversational fluency. You can't expect this until you go abroad and live in a country for a period of time. What it will give you very rapidly is the ability to survive in a large number of situations you will meet abroad. Once you have gotten this framework, you will find it much easier to pick up more words and grammar when you travel.

IMPORTANT NOTE

The first section of the course can be basically regarded as a training section designed to get you into the By Association method quickly and easily.

After about forty-five minutes, you will have a vocabulary of about thirty words and be able to translate sentences. Once you have finished Section 1, you will have the confidence to go through the rest of the course just as quickly. Animal words are used in the first section since they are a large group of "easy to image" words. Many animal words of course are useful to have as they are often met abroad, e.g., dog, cat, etc., or they are edible!

Finally, when it comes to translating sentences, the answers are given at the bottom of the page. You may find it useful to cover up the answers before you try to do the translations.

SECTION 1

ANIMALS

☐ **Think of each image in your mind's eye for about ten seconds.**
For example, the French for **tablecloth** is **nappe.** Imagine in your mind's eye for ten seconds having a **nap** on a tablecloth.

☐ *Note: The word on the right-hand side of the page*
(IN PARENTHESES) is the way the word is pronounced.

SOME ANIMALS

- The French for **rabbit** is **lapin.** (LAPAHn)*
  Imagine a rabbit **lapping** at a bowl of water.

- The French for **cat** is **chat.** (SHA)
  Imagine a cat **shat**tering a glass.

- The French for **goat** is **chèvre.** (SHEVR)
  Imagine driving your **Chevy** to the levee with a goat in the back.

- The French for **horse** is **cheval.** (SHeVAL)
  Imagine you prod a horse with a **shovel.**

- The French for **animal** is **animal.** (ANEEMAL)
  Imagine **animals** looking out from the Eiffel Tower.

- The French for **cow** is **vache.** (VASH)
  Imagine trying to **wash** a cow.

- The French for **dog** is **chien.** (SHEE AHn)
  Imagine a dog with a **shine** on its coat.

- The French for **deer** is **cerf.** (SER)
  Imagine you **ser**ve a deer dinner.

- The French for **goose** is **oie.** (WA)
  Imagine a goose hanging from a **wire** in a butcher's shop.

*Remember that a small *n* in the pronunciation always sounds like the *n* in *fiancé.*

7

☐ *You can write your answers in*

- What is the English for **oie**? (WA)

- What is the English for **cerf**? (SER) _____

- What is the English for **chien**? (SHEE AHn) _____

- What is the English for **vache**? (VASH) _____

- What is the English for **animal**? (ANEEMAL) _____

- What is the English for **cheval**? (SHeVAL)* _____

- What is the English for **chèvre**? (SHEVR) _____

- What is the English for **chat**? (SHA) _____

- What is the English for **lapin**? (LAPAHn) _____

← *Look back for the answers*

ELEMENTARY GRAMMAR

All nouns in French are either *masculine* or *feminine*, even though they may be things.

Because you cannot tell whether a word is masculine or feminine just by listening to it, you will now be shown how to remember the gender of words in French.

☐ If the word is *masculine*, always associate it in your mind's eye with a boxer.

➜ *For example,*

- **rabbit** is *masculine* in French:
  Imagine a boxer punching a rabbit.

  Every time you see a word with a boxer, you will know that it is *masculine*.

☐ If the word is *feminine*, always imagine the word interacting with a bottle of French perfume.

➜ *For example,*

- **cow** is *feminine* in French.
  Imagine a cow with a bottle of perfume dangling from her neck.

  When you see a bottle of perfume in your mind's eye interacting with a word, you will know the word is *feminine* in French.

Masculine Nouns

The French for *the* when the noun is masculine is *le* (pronounced Le).

➜ *For example,*

- *the dog* is *le chien*

- *the cat* is *le chat*

Feminine Nouns

The French for *the* when the noun is feminine is *la* (pronounced LA).

➜ *For example,*

- *the cow* is *la vache*

- *the goat* is *la chèvre*

   Imagine thinking "Ooh! *La!* La! what a beautiful cow."

Plurals

If the French is plural, then the word for *the* is always *les* (pronounced LAY).

Finally, if a word starts with a vowel (like *animal*), then the word for *the* is *l'* (for example, *l'animal* or *l'oie*) no matter what the gender.

GENDERS

☐ **Think of each image in your mind's eye for about ten seconds**

- The gender of **rabbit** is *masculine*.
  Imagine a boxer punching a rabbit.   **le lapin**

- The gender of **cat** is *masculine*.
  Imagine a boxer with a cat on his knee.   **le chat**

- The gender of **goat** is *feminine*.
  Imagine pouring a bottle of perfume over a goat
  to stop the smell.   **la chèvre**

- The gender of **horse** is *masculine*.
  Imagine a boxer riding to the ring on a horse.   **le cheval**

- The gender of **animal** is *masculine*.
  Imagine a boxer in a ring surrounded by
  animals.   **l'animal**

- The gender of **cow** is *feminine*.
  Imagine a cow with a bottle of perfume
  dangling from her neck instead of a bell.   **la vache**

- The gender of **dog** is *masculine*.
  Imagine a boxer dog with a boxer.   **le chien**

- The gender of **deer** is *masculine*.
  Imagine a boxer with a deer slung over his
  shoulder.   **le cerf**

- The gender of **goose** is *feminine*.
  Imagine a goose pecking at a bottle of perfume.   **l'oie**

☐ *You can write your answers in*

- What is the gender and French for **goose**?   _____

- What is the gender and French for **deer**?   _____

- What is the gender and French for **dog**?   _____

- What is the gender and French for **cow**?   _____

- What is the gender and French for **animal**?   _____

- What is the gender and French for **horse**?   _____

- What is the gender and French for **goat**?   _____

- What is the gender and French for **cat**?   _____

- What is the gender and French for **rabbit**?   _____

← *Look back for the answers*

SOME MORE ANIMALS

☐ **Think of each image in your mind's eye for about ten seconds**

- The French for **fish** is **poisson.**   (PWASOHn)
  Imagine that you **poison** your pet fish.

- The French for **trout** is **truite.**   (TRWEET)
  Imagine eating a beautiful trout—a **true eat.**

- The French for **lobster** is **homard.**   (OMAR)
  Imagine the famous actor **Omar** Sharif eating a
  huge lobster.

- The French for **sheep** is **mouton.**   (MOOTOHn)
  Imagine getting **mutton** from a live sheep.

- The French for **mouse** is **souris.**   (SOOREE)
  Imagine a mouse running through a **sewer.**

- The French for **oyster** is **huître.**   (WEETR)
  Imagine throwing an oyster into a **wheat** field.

- The French for **wasp** is **guêpe.**   (GEP)
  Imagine a wasp flying through a **gap** in a wall.

- The French for **hen** is **poule.**   (POOL)
  Imagine a hen in a **pool** of water.

- The French for **duck** is **canard.**   (KANAR)
  Imagine someone who cans dead ducks—a duck
  canner.

- What is the English for **canard**? (KANAR)   ————————

- What is the English for **poule**? (POOL)   ————————

- What is the English for **guêpe**? (GEP)   ————————

- What is the English for **huître**? (WEETR)   ————————

- What is the English for **souris**? (SOOREE)   ————————

- What is the English for **mouton**? (MOOTOHn)   ————————

- What is the English for **homard**? (OMAR)   ————————

- What is the English for **truite**? (TRWEET)   ————————

- What is the English for **poisson**? (PWASOHn)   ————————

← *Look back for the answers*

14

GENDERS

☐ **Think of each image in your mind's eye for about ten seconds**

- The gender of **fish** is *masculine*.   **le poisson**
  Imagine a boxer fishing for fish.

- The gender of **trout** is *feminine*.   **la truite**
  Imagine a trout cooked in a perfumed sauce.

- The gender of **lobster** is *masculine*.   **le homard**
  Imagine a boxer digging into a delicious meal
  of lobster.

- The gender of **sheep** is *masculine*.   **le mouton**
  Imagine a boxer bringing his pet sheep into the
  ring.

- The gender of **mouse** is *feminine*.   **la souris**
  Imagine drowning a little mouse in a bottle of
  perfume.

- The gender of **oyster** is *feminine*.   **l'huître**
  Imagine oysters dipped in perfume before being
  swallowed.

- The gender of **wasp** is *feminine*.   **la guêpe**
  Imagine wasps swarming around a bottle of
  perfume.

- The gender of **hen** is *feminine*.   **la poule***
  Imagine a hen pecking at a bottle of perfume.

- The gender of **duck** is *masculine*.   **le canard**
  Imagine a boxer shooing ducks out of the
  boxing ring.

*Note: **Chicken** is **le poulet**.

15

☐ *You can write your answers in*

- What is the gender and French for **duck**? _____

- What is the gender and French for **hen**? _____

- What is the gender and French for **wasp**? _____

- What is the gender and French for **oyster**? _____

- What is the gender and French for **mouse**? _____

- What is the gender and French for **sheep**? _____

- What is the gender and French for **lobster**? _____

- What is the gender and French for **trout**? _____

- What is the gender and French for **fish**? _____

← *Look back for the answers*

USEFUL WORDS

This page will deal with some useful words which do not have any genders for you to remember.

☐ **Think of each image in your mind's eye for about ten seconds**

- The French for **tired** is **fatigué.**   (FATEEGAY)
  Imagine being tired and **fatigued.**

- The French for **quick** is **rapide.**   (RAPEED)
  Imagine being quick and **rapid.**

- The French for **quiet** is **tranquille.**   (TROnKEEL)
  Imagine everything being quiet and **tranquil.**

- The French for **big** is **grand.**   (GROn)
  Imagine something being big and **grand.**

- The French for **small** is **petit.**   (PeTEE)
  Imagine a **petite** little girl.

- The French for **heavy** is **lourd.**   (LOOR)
  Imagine you **lure** a heavy man to his doom.

- The French for **thin** is **mince.**   (MAHnS)
  Imagine having a ro**mance** with a thin partner.

- The French for **dirty** is **sale.**   (SAL)
  Imagine eating a very dirty **sal**ad.

☐ *You can write your answers in*

- What is the English for **sale**? (SAL)　　　　　＿＿＿＿＿＿＿＿

- What is the English for **mince**? (MAHnS)　＿＿＿＿＿＿＿＿

- What is the English for **lourd**? (LOOR)　　＿＿＿＿＿＿＿＿

- What is the English for **petit**? (PeTEE)　　＿＿＿＿＿＿＿＿

- What is the English for **grand**? (GROn)　　＿＿＿＿＿＿＿＿

- What is the English for **tranquille**?　　　　＿＿＿＿＿＿＿＿
  (TROnKEEL)

- What is the English for **rapide**? (RAPEED)　＿＿＿＿＿＿＿＿

- What is the English for **fatigué**?　　　　　＿＿＿＿＿＿＿＿
  (FATEEGAY)

← *Look back for the answers*

18

☐ *You can write your answers in*

- What is the French for **dirty**? _____

- What is the French for **thin**? _____

- What is the French for **heavy**? _____

- What is the French for **small**? _____

- What is the French for **big**? _____

- What is the French for **quiet**? _____

- What is the French for **quick**? _____

- What is the French for **tired**? _____

← *Look back for the answers*

ELEMENTARY GRAMMAR

The French for *is* is *est* (pronounced EH).

To say

>   *the dog is quick*

you simply say

>   *le chien est rapide.*

Please note: *Est* is pronounced "ET" when it comes before a vowel.

Now cover up the answers below and translate the following:

☐ *(You can write your answers in)*

1. The dog is small.

2. The deer is tired.

3. The horse is big.

4. The lobster is dirty.

5. The cat is heavy.

_____

_____

_____

_____

_____

_____

_____

_____

☐ *The answers are:*

1. Le chien est petit.

2. Le cerf est fatigué.

3. Le cheval est grand.

4. Le homard est sale.

5. Le chat est lourd.

Now cover up the answers below and translate the following:

☐ *(You can write your answers in)*

1. La chèvre est mince.

2. L'huître est rapide.

3. Le mouton est petit.

4. Le lapin est grand.

5. Le canard est sale.

_____

_____

_____

_____

_____

_____

_____

_____

☐ *The answers are:*

1. The goat is thin.

2. The oyster is quick.

3. The sheep is small.

4. The rabbit is big.

5. The duck is dirty.

IMPORTANT NOTE

Some of the sentences in this course might strike you as being a bit odd!

However, they have been carefully constructed to make you think much more about what you are translating. This helps the memory process and gets away from the idea of learning useful phrases "parrot fashion."

But of course, having learned with the help of these seemingly odd sentences, you can easily construct your own sentences to suit your particular needs.

SECTION 2

HOME, FURNITURE, COLORS

FURNITURE

☐ **Think of each image in your mind's eye for about ten seconds**

- The French for **table** is **table.** (TABL)
  Imagine throwing a **table** from the top of the
  Eiffel Tower.

- The French for **chair** is **chaise.** (SHEZ)
  Imagine you have **shares** in a chair.

- The French for **cupboard** is **placard.** (PLAKAR)
  Imagine a **placard** stuck to a cupboard.

- The French for **wardrobe** is **armoire.** (ARMWAR)
  Imagine your **arm worn** out by trying to open a
  wardrobe door that is stuck.

- The French for **clock** is **pendule.** (POnDooL)
  Imagine a grandfather clock with a large
  pendulum.

- The French for **bed** is **lit.** (LEE)
  Imagine you **lay** on a bed.

- The French for **piano** is **piano.** (PEE ANOH)
  Imagine playing a **piano** at the top of the Eiffel
  Tower.

- The French for **curtain** is **rideau.** (REEDOH)
  Imagine having to **re-do** the curtains after you
  have made a mess of them.

- The French for **armchair** is **fauteuil.** (FOTOEY)
  Imagine taking a **photo** of an armchair.

- The French for **carpet** is **tapis.** (TAPEE)
  Imagine your carpet under a **tapestry.**

☐ *You can write your answers in*

- What is the English for **tapis**? (TAPEE) _____

- What is the English for **fauteuil**? (FOTOEY) _____

- What is the English for **rideau**? (REEDOH) _____

- What is the English for **piano**? (PEE ANOH) _____

- What is the English for **lit**? (LEE) _____

- What is the English for **pendule**? (POnDooL) _____

- What is the English for **armoire**? (ARMWAR) _____

- What is the English for **placard**? (PLAKAR) _____

- What is the English for **chaise**? (SHEZ) _____

- What is the English for **table**? (TABL) _____

← *Look back for the answers*

☐ **Think of each image in your mind's eye for about ten seconds**

- The gender of **table** is *feminine*.   **la table**
  Imagine a large bottle of perfume on the table.

- The gender of **chair** is *feminine*.   **la chaise**
  Imagine spilling perfume on a chair to make it
  smell better.

- The gender of **cupboard** is *masculine*.   **le placard**
  Imagine a boxer punching a cupboard.

- The gender of **wardrobe** is *feminine*.   **l'armoire**
  Imagine spilling perfume onto your wardrobe to
  stop the smell of mothballs.

- The gender of **clock** is *feminine*.   **la pendule**
  Imagine a bottle of perfume at the bottom of the
  pendulum of a clock.

- The gender of **bed** is *masculine*.   **le lit**
  Imagine putting a boxer to bed after a bad fight.

- The gender of **piano** is *masculine*.   **le piano**
  Imagine a boxer trying to play the piano with
  boxing gloves on.

- The gender of **curtain** is *masculine*.   **le rideau**
  Imagine a boxer climbing up a curtain.

- The gender of **armchair** is *masculine*.   **le fauteuil**
  Imagine a boxer slumped in your favorite
  armchair.

- The gender of **carpet** is *masculine*.   **le tapis**
  Imagine a carpeted boxing ring, with a boxer
  lying on the carpet.

- What is the gender and French for **carpet**? _____

- What is the gender and French for **armchair**? _____

- What is the gender and French for **curtain**? _____

- What is the gender and French for **piano**? _____

- What is the gender and French for **bed**? _____

- What is the gender and French for **clock**? _____

- What is the gender and French for **wardrobe**? _____

- What is the gender and French for **cupboard**? _____

- What is the gender and French for **chair**? _____

- What is the gender and French for **table**? _____

← *Look back for the answers*

SOME HOUSE WORDS

☐ **Think of each image in your mind's eye for about ten seconds**

- The French for **door** is **porte.** (PORT)
  Imagine a **port** with a huge door at the entrance.

- The French for **window** is **fenêtre.** (FeNETR)
  Imagine covering windows with a **fine net.**

- The French for **garden** is **jardin.** (JARDAHn)
  Imagine a **garden** on the top of the Eiffel Tower.

- The French for **roof** is **toit.** (TWA)
  Imagine a **twan**ging noise on the roof.

- The French for **ceiling** is **plafond.** (PLAFOHn)
  Imagine using a **platform** to paint the ceiling.

- The French for **staircase** is **escalier.** (ESKALEE AY)
  Imagine your staircase is like an **escalator.**

- The French for **floor** is **plancher.** (PLOnSHAY)
  Imagine **plunging** through rotten floors.

- The French for **wall** is **mur.** (MooR)
  Imagine a **mural** painted on your wall.

- The French for **kitchen** is **cuisine.** (KWEEZEEN)
  Imagine preparing beautiful **cuisine** in your kitchen.

- The French for **room** is **pièce.** (PEE ES)
  Imagine someone writing to you to say, "**P.S.** Your room will be very small."

- What is the English for **pièce**? (PEE ES) _____

- What is the English for **cuisine**? (KWEEZEEN) _____

- What is the English for **mur**? (MooR) _____

- What is the English for **plancher**? (PLOnSHAY) _____

- What is the English for **escalier**? (ESKALEE AY) _____

- What is the English for **plafond**? (PLAFOHn) _____

- What is the English for **toit**? (TWA) _____

- What is the English for **jardin**? (JARDAHn) _____

- What is the English for **fenêtre**? (FeNETR) _____

- What is the English for **porte**? (PORT) _____

← *Look back for the answers*

☐ **Think of each image in your mind's eye for about ten seconds**

- The gender of **door** is *feminine*.
  Imagine a bottle of perfume used as a door
  knocker on a door.   **la porte**

- The gender of **window** is *feminine*.
  Imagine spraying a window with perfume and
  using it as a window cleaner.   **la fenêtre**

- The gender of **garden** is *masculine*.
  Imagine a boxing match in your garden.   **le jardin**

- The gender of **roof** is *masculine*.
  Imagine two boxers fighting on a roof.   **le toit**

- The gender of **ceiling** is *masculine*.
  Imagine a boxer being punched so hard he
  bangs his head on the ceiling.   **le plafond**

- The gender of **staircase** is *masculine*.
  Imagine a boxer falling down some stairs.   **l'escalier**

- The gender of **floor** is *masculine*.
  Imagine a boxer on the floor.   **le plancher**

- The gender of **wall** is *masculine*.
  Imagine a boxer sitting on a wall.   **le mur**

- The gender of **kitchen** is *feminine*.
  Imagine spraying your kitchen with perfume to
  hide bad smells.   **la cuisine**

- The gender of **room** is *feminine*.
  Imagine a room stacked full of bottles of
  perfume.   **la pièce**

□ *You can write your answers in*

- What is the gender and French for **room**? _____

- What is the gender and French for **kitchen**? _____

- What is the gender and French for **wall**? _____

- What is the gender and French for **floor**? _____

- What is the gender and French for **stairs**? _____

- What is the gender and French for **ceiling**? _____

- What is the gender and French for **roof**? _____

- What is the gender and French for **garden**? _____

- What is the gender and French for **window**? _____

- What is the gender and French for **door**? _____

← *Look back for the answers*

COLORS

☐ **Think of each image in your mind's eye for about ten seconds**

- The French for **black** is **noir.**   (NWAR)
  Imagine someone telling you "There is **no r** in black."

- The French for **white** is **blanc.**   (BLOn)
  Imagine a **blonde** girl in a white dress.

- The French for **red** is **rouge.**   (ROOJ)
  Imagine someone whose face is reddened with **rouge.**

- The French for **yellow** is **jaune.**   (JON)
  Imagine someone yellow from **jaundice.**

- The French for **green** is **vert.**   (VER)
  Imagine someone with a **very** green face.

- The French for **blue** is **bleu.**   (BLe)
  Imagine painting the Eiffel Tower blue.

- The French for **pink** is **rose.**   (ROZ)
  Imagine a pink **rose.**

- The French for **orange** is **orange.**   (OROnJ)
  Imagine painting the Eiffel Tower a bright **orange.**

- The French for **gold(en)** is **doré.**   (DORAY)
  Imagine a gold **door.**

- The French for **gray** is **gris.**   (GREE)
  Imagine gray-colored **grease.**

☐ *You can write your answers in*

- What is the English for **gris**? (GREE) _____

- What is the English for **doré**? (DORAY) _____

- What is the English for **orange**? (OROnJ) _____

- What is the English for **rose**? (ROZ) _____

- What is the English for **bleu**? (BLe) _____

- What is the English for **vert**? (VER) _____

- What is the English for **jaune**? (JON) _____

- What is the English for **rouge**? (ROOJ) _____

- What is the English for **blanc**? (BLOn) _____

- What is the English for **noir**? (NWAR) _____

← *Look back for the answers*

You can write your answers in

- What is the French for **gray**?   —————————

- What is the French for **gold(en)**?   —————————

- What is the French for **orange**?   —————————

- What is the French for **pink**?   —————————

- What is the French for **blue**?   —————————

- What is the French for **green**?   —————————

- What is the French for **yellow**?   —————————

- What is the French for **red**?   —————————

- What is the French for **white**?   —————————

- What is the French for **black**?   —————————

← *Look back for the answers*

ELEMENTARY GRAMMAR

In French, adjectives (like *big*, *dirty*, etc.) change their endings to agree with the gender of the word they go with.

When the word is *feminine*, then you normally add an *e* to the end of the adjective.

➡ *For example,*

- *petit chien* (masculine) is *little dog*

- *petite chèvre* (feminine) is *little goat*

- *grand tapis* (masculine) is *big carpet*

- *grande table* (feminine) is *big table*

In the *masculine*, the last consonant is not normally pronounced.

So, *petit* is pronounced PeTEE.

However, in the *feminine*, you do pronounce the last consonant.

So, *petite* is pronounced PeTEET.

Again, *grand* is pronounced GROn.
  grande is pronounced GROnD.

If, however, the adjective already ends in *e* (for example, *rapide, sale,* etc.), then you make no change in either spelling or pronunciation in the feminine.

Please note these *feminine* forms:

- *white* is *blanche* (BLOnSH)

- *gray* is *grise* (GREEZ)

Now cover up the answers below and translate the following:

□ *(You can write your answers in)*

1. The chair is pink.

2. The wardrobe is blue.

3. The cupboard is green.

4. The bed is heavy.

5. The goose is tired.

_____

_____

_____

_____

_____

_____

_____

□ *The answers are:*

1. La chaise est rose.
2. L'armoire est bleue.
3. Le placard est vert.
4. Le lit est lourd.
5. L'oie est fatiguée.

☐ **Now cover up the answers below and translate the following:**

☐ *(You can write your answers in)*

1. Le piano est blanc.

2. Le tapis est sale.

3. Le rideau est doré.

4. Le fauteuil est grand.

5. L'escalier est lourd.

_____

_____

_____

_____

_____

_____

_____

☐ *The answers are:*

1. The piano is white.
2. The carpet is dirty.
3. The curtain is gold(en).
4. The armchair is big.
5. The staircase is heavy.

SOME USEFUL WORDS FOR MAKING SENTENCES

☐ **Think of each image in your mind's eye for about ten seconds**

- The French for **eats** is **mange.**   (MOnJ)*
  Imagine **eat**ing blanc**mange.**

- The French for **has** is **a.**   (A)
  Imagine someone **has a** something or other.

- The French for **wants** is **veut.**   (Ve)
  Imagine you **want** a **fur** coat.

- The French for **sees** is **voit.**   (VWA)
  Imagine a German saying, "I **see vwat**er in the sea."

☐ *You can write your answers in*

- What is the English for **voit**? (VWA)   _____

- What is the English for **veut**? (Ve)   _____

- What is the English for **a**? (A)   _____

- What is the English for **mange**? (MOnJ)   _____

← *Look back for the answers*

☐ *You can write your answers in*

- What is the French for **sees**? _____

- What is the French for **wants**? _____

- What is the French for **has**? _____

- What is the French for **eats**? _____

← *Look back for the answers*

ELEMENTARY GRAMMAR

Adjectives in French often come after the noun.

➜ *For example,*

- *black dog* is *chien noir*

- *quick cat* is *chat rapide*

With one or two exceptions, it is not wrong to put the adjectives you have already been given after the noun.

➜ *For example,*

- *red table* is *table rouge*

- *quiet cow* is *vache tranquille*

The two exceptions among the words you have just learned are:

- *big* — *grand*

- *small* — *petit*

These two words almost always come *before* the noun.

➜ *For example,*

- *big rabbit* is *grand lapin*

- *small chair* is *petite chaise*

☐ **Now cover up the answers below and translate the following:**

☐ *(You can write your answers in)*

1. The black horse eats the green chair.

2. The little mouse sees the big deer.

3. The quick trout has the red lobster.

4. The tired animal wants the gray bed.

5. The yellow clock is big.

_____

_____

_____

_____

_____

_____

_____

☐ *The answers are:*

1. Le cheval noir mange la chaise verte.

2. La petite souris voit le grand cerf.

3. La truite rapide a le homard rouge.

4. L'animal fatigué veut le lit gris.

5. La pendule jaune est grande.

1. La petite vache voit la porte noire.

2. Le mur vert est sale.

3. La chèvre fatiguée veut la fenêtre bleue.

4. L'oie rapide mange le toit orange.

5. Le chat noir a le plancher rouge.

_____

_____

_____

_____

_____

_____

_____

□ *The answers are:*

1. The little cow sees the black door.
2. The green wall is dirty.
3. The tired goat wants the blue window.
4. The quick goose eats the orange roof.
5. The black cat has the red floor.

SECTION 3

CLOTHES

☐ **Think of each image in your mind's eye for about ten seconds**

- The French for **clothes** is **vêtements.** (VETMOn)
  Imagine that you explain to your mother,
  "I took all my clothes to the **vet, ma.**"

- The French for **underpants** is **slip.** (SLEEP)
  Imagine you **sleep** in your underpants.

- The French for **trousers** (pants) is **pantalon.** (POnTALOHn)
  Imagine your trousers are baggy **pantaloons.**

- The French for **skirt** is **jupe.** (JooP)
  Imagine spilling **soup** on your skirt.

- The French for **sock** is **chaussette.** (SHOSET)
  Imagine you buy a magnificent pair of socks—
  they are a **show set.**

- The French for **jacket** is **veste.** (VEST)
  Imagine you wear a **vest** while everybody else
  is wearing a smart jacket to a dance.

- The French for **dress** is **robe.** (ROB)
  Imagine someone **robs** you of your best dress.

- The French for **pullover** is **pullover.** (PooLOVER)
  Imagine taking your **pullover** off at the top of
  the Eiffel Tower.

- The French for **shoe** is **chaussure.** (SHOSooR)
  Imagine an usher saying, "You can't get into
  the **show, sir,** unless you wear shoes."

- The French for **hat** is **chapeau.** (SHAPOH)
  Imagine taking off your hat when you enter a
  chapel.

- What is the English for **chapeau**?
(SHAPOH)

- What is the English for **chaussure**?
(SHOSooR)

- What is the English for **pullover**?
(PooLOVER)

- What is the English for **robe**? (ROB)

- What is the English for **veste**? (VEST)

- What is the English for **chaussette**?
(SHOSET)

- What is the English for **jupe**? (JooP)

- What is the English for **pantalon**?
(POnTALOHn)

- What is the English for **slip**? (SLEEP)

- What is the English for **vêtements**?
(VETMOn)

← *Look back for the answers*

☐ **Think of each image in your mind's eye for about ten seconds**

- The gender of **vêtements** is *masculine*.
  Imagine a boxer putting clothes on after a fight.
  (Note: This is a plural word. The word for *the*
  in the plural is *les*.)

  les vêtements

- The gender of **underpants** is *masculine*.
  Imagine a boxer fighting in his underpants.

  le slip

- The gender of **trousers** (pants) is *masculine*.
  Imagine a boxer pulling on his trousers after a
  fight.

  le pantalon

- The gender of **skirt** is *feminine*.
  Imagine spilling perfume on a skirt.

  la jupe

- The gender of **sock** is *feminine*.
  Imagine spraying perfume on your socks to kill
  the smell.

  la chaussette

- The gender of **jacket** is *feminine*.
  Imagine spraying your jacket with perfume to
  make it smell nice.

  la veste

- The gender of **dress** is *feminine*.
  Imagine spilling a bottle of perfume all over a
  dress.

  la robe

- The gender of **pullover** is *masculine*.
  Imagine a boxer wearing a pullover during a
  fight.

  le pullover

- The gender of **shoe** is *feminine*.
  Imagine spraying the top of your shoe with
  perfume to improve the smell.

  la chaussure

- The gender of **hat** is *masculine*.
  Imagine a boxer having a hat knocked off his
  head in a fight.

  le chapeau

- What is the gender and French for **hat**? _____

- What is the gender and French for **shoe**? _____

- What is the gender and French for **pullover**? _____

- What is the gender and French for **dress**? _____

- What is the gender and French for **jacket**? _____

- What is the gender and French for **sock**? _____

- What is the gender and French for **skirt**? _____

- What is the gender and French for **trousers**? _____

- What is the gender and French for **underpants**? _____

- What is the gender and French for **clothes**? _____

← *Look back for the answers*

ELEMENTARY GRAMMAR

☐ The French word for *I* is *je* (pronounced Je).

The French word for *am* is *suis* (pronounced SWEE). Imagine I am a *Swede*.

To say *I am* (e.g., *I am the dog*), you say *Je suis le chien*.

To say *I am the door,* you say *Je suis la porte*.

☐ The French word for *he* is *il* (pronounced EEL). Imagine he is in an *eel*.

→ *So,*

- *he is*   is *il est*

- *he eats*   is *il mange*

- *he is tired* is *il est fatigué*

☐ The French word for *she* is *elle* (pronounced EL). Imagine she is *well* dressed.

→ *So,*

- *she sees*   is *elle voit*

- *she is dirty* is *elle est sale*

☐ **Now cover up the answers below and translate the following:**

☐ *(You can write your answers in)*

1. He sees the blue jacket.

2. I am the big cat.

3. She has the heavy pullover.

4. He wants the yellow sock.

5. She eats the red shoe.

_____

_____

_____

_____

_____

_____

_____

_____

☐ *The answers are:*

1. Il voit la veste bleue.

2. Je suis le grand chat.

3. Elle a le pullover lourd.

4. Il veut la chaussette jaune.

5. Elle mange la chaussure rouge.

Now cover up the answers below and translate the following:

☐ *(You can write your answers in)*

1. Il voit le plafond rose.

2. Elle veut la jupe sale.

3. Je suis l'animal noir.

4. Il mange la robe grise.

5. Elle a les vêtements jaunes.

Please note that with this last sentence you add an *s* to the adjective.

This will be dealt with more fully later on.

_____

_____

_____

_____

_____

_____

☐ *The answers are:*

1. He sees the pink ceiling.
2. She wants the dirty skirt.
3. I am the black animal.
4. He eats the gray dress.
5. She has the yellow clothes.

FAMILY WORDS

☐ **Think of each image in your mind's eye for about ten seconds**

- The French for **father** is **père.**   (PER)
  Imagine your father is your **par**ent.

- The French for **mother** is **mère.**   (MER)
  Imagine your mother mounted on a gray **mare.**

- The French for **brother** is **frère.**   (FRER)
  Imagine your brother dressed up as a holy **friar.**

- The French for **sister** is **soeur.**   (SeR)
  Imagine your sister saying, "Hello, **sir.**"

- The French for **husband** is **mari.**   (MAREE)
  Imagine you **marry** your husband.

- The French for **wife** is **femme.**   (FAM)
  Imagine wives as the tallest members of the
  family.
  (Note: *Femme* is the same as the word for
  woman.)

- The French for **son** is **fils.**   (FEES)
  Imagine having to pay school **fees** for your son.

- The French for **daughter** is **fille.**   (FEE)
  Imagine selling your daughter for a **fee.**

- The French for **boy** is **garçon.**   (GARSOHn)
  Imagine a young boy has left the **gas on,** and
  the soup burned.
  (Note: *Garçon* is the same as the word for
  waiter.)

- The French for **girl** is **jeune fille.**   (JeN FEE)
  Imagine a girl on a **young filly.**

- What is the English for **jeune fille**?
  (JeN FEE)
  _____

- What is the English for **garçon**?
  (GARSOHn)
  _____

- What is the English for **fille**? (FEE)
  _____

- What is the English for **fils**? (FEES)
  _____

- What is the English for **femme**? (FAM)
  _____

- What is the English for **mari**? (MAREE)
  _____

- What is the English for **soeur**? (SeR)
  _____

- What is the English for **frère**? (FRER)
  _____

- What is the English for **mère**? (MER)
  _____

- What is the English for **père**? (PER)
  _____

← *Look back for the answers*

☐ *You can write your answers in*

The genders of family words are given by the sex of the person.

- What is the gender and French for **girl**? _____

- What is the gender and French for **boy**? _____

- What is the gender and French for _____
  daughter?

- What is the gender and French for **son**? _____

- What is the gender and French for **wife**? _____

- What is the gender and French for _____
  husband?

- What is the gender and French for **sister**? _____

- What is the gender and French for _____
  brother?

- What is the gender and French for **mother**? _____

- What is the gender and French for **father**? _____

← *Look back for the answers*

SOME MORE USEFUL WORDS

☐ **Think of each image in your mind's eye for about ten seconds**

- The French for **empty** is **vide.**　　　　(VEED)
  Imagine a German putting a **veed** (weed) into
  an empty jar.

- The French for **deep** is **profond.**　　　(PROFOHn)
  Imagine thinking deep, **profound** thoughts.

- The French for **ugly** is **laid.**　　　　　(LAY)
  Imagine an ugly duckling **lay**ing an egg.

- The French for **expensive** is **cher.**　　　(SHER)
  Imagine you **share** the cost of an expensive
  meal.

- The French for **cold** is **froid.**　　　　　(FRWA)
  Imagine you **fry** a cold sausage.

- The French for **hot** is **chaud.**　　　　　(SHOH)
  Imagine you try hard not to **show** how hot you
  are.

- The French for **pretty** is **joli.**　　　　(JOLEE)
  Imagine a **jolly,** pretty girl.

- What is the English for **joli**? (JOLEE) _____

- What is the English for **chaud**? (SHOH) _____

- What is the English for **froid**? (FRWA) _____

- What is the English for **cher**? (SHER) _____

- What is the English for **laid**? (LAY) _____

- What is the English for **profond**? (PROFOHn) _____

- What is the English for **vide**? (VEED) _____

← *Look back for the answers*

☐ *You can write your answers in*

- What is the French for **pretty**? _____

- What is the French for **hot**? _____

- What is the French for **cold**? _____

- What is the French for **expensive**? _____

- What is the French for **ugly**? _____

- What is the French for **deep**? _____

- What is the French for **empty**? _____

← *Look back for the answers*

ELEMENTARY GRAMMAR

☐ The French for *and* is *et* (pronounced AY like AID). Imagine *a* and *b*.

➔ *So,*

- *hot and cold* is *chaud et froid*

- *red and green* is *rouge et vert*

☐ The French for *but* is *mais* (pronounced MAY). Imagine you like any month but *May.*

➔ *So,*

- *pretty but expensive* is *joli mais cher*

- *small but quiet*   is *petit mais tranquille*

☐ The French for *or* is *ou* (pronounced OO). Imagine people say "*Ooh!* or ah!"

➔ *So,*

- *the dog or the cat* is *le chien ou le chat*

- *the wall or the floor* is *le mur ou le plancher*

☐ **Now cover up the answers below and translate the following:**

☐ *(You can write your answers in)*

1. He eats the rabbit and the dog.

2. She wants the kitchen or the garden.

3. I am small but heavy.

4. She is quiet and thin, but pretty.

5. The room is empty and the kitchen is black.

_____

_____

_____

_____

_____

_____

_____

_____

☐ *The answers are:*

1. Il mange le lapin et le chien.

2. Elle veut la cuisine ou le jardin.

3. Je suis petit mais lourd.

4. Elle est tranquille et mince, mais jolie.

5. La pièce est vide et la cuisine est noire.

□ **Now cover up the answers below and translate the following:**

□ *(You can write your answers in)*

1. Il est le père et elle est la mère.

2. Je suis le frère sale, mais la soeur est lourde.

3. La jeune fille mange le grand fils.

4. Il veut le joli mari ou la femme laide.
   (Note: *Joli* normally comes before the noun.)

5. Le père est laid et la mère est grande.

_____

_____

_____

_____

_____

_____

_____

□ *The answers are:*

1. He is the father and she is the mother.

2. I am the dirty brother, but the sister is heavy.

3. The girl eats the big son.

4. He wants the pretty husband or the ugly wife.

5. The father is ugly and the mother is big.

SECTION 4

IN THE COUNTRY, TIME WORDS, NUMBERS

TRAVELING IN THE COUNTRY

☐ **Think of each image in your mind's eye for about ten seconds**

- The French for **grass** is **herbe.**   (ERB)
  Imagine you use grass as an **herb** to cure your
  sore leg.

- The French for **flower** is **fleur.**   (FLeR)
  Imagine throwing **flowers** from the top of the
  Eiffel Tower.

- The French for **tree** is **arbre.**   (ARBR)
  Imagine a tree-lined **harbor.**

- The French for **fruit** is **fruit.**   (FRWEE)
  Imagine getting some **free** fruit.

- The French for **fly** is **mouche.**   (MOOSH)
  Imagine you catch flies and **mush** them up.

- The French for **insect** is **insecte.**   (AHnSEKT)
  Imagine an **insect** crawling up the Eiffel Tower.

- What is the English for **insecte**?
  (AHnSEKT)
  _____

- What is the English for **mouche**?
  (MOOSH)
  _____

- What is the English for **fruit**? (FRWEE)
  _____

- What is the English for **arbre**? (ARBR)
  _____

- What is the English for **fleur**? (FLeR)
  _____

- What is the English for **herbe**? (ERB)
  _____

← *Look back for the answers*

☐ Think of each image in your mind's eye for about ten seconds

- The gender of **grass** is *feminine*.
  Imagine spraying grass with perfume. **l'herbe**

- The gender of **flower** is *feminine*.
  Imagine making flowers into perfume. **la fleur**

- The gender of **tree** is *masculine*.
  Imagine a boxer using a tree as a punching bag. **l'arbre**

- The gender of **fruit** is *masculine*.
  Imagine a boxer eating a bag of fruit just before
  he gets up to fight. **le fruit**

- The gender of **fly** is *feminine*.
  Imagine spraying flies with a deadly perfume. **la mouche**

- The gender of **insect** is *masculine*.
  Imagine a boxer stamping on all sorts of insects
  in the ring. **l'insecte**

☐ *You can write your answers in*

- What is the gender and French for **insect**?   _____

- What is the gender and French for **fly**?   _____

- What is the gender and French for **fruit**?   _____

- What is the gender and French for **tree**?   _____

- What is the gender and French for **flower**?   _____

- What is the gender and French for **grass**?   _____

← *Look back for the answers*

ELEMENTARY GRAMMAR

If you want to say *a dog, a bed*, etc., then the word for *a* is *un* (pronounced "en," something like the English *earn*).

→ *So,*

- *a dog* is *un chien*

- *a bed* is *un lit*

For feminine words like *a cow, a flower,* etc., the word for *a* is *une* (pronounced ooN).

→ *So,*

- *a cow* is *une vache*

- *a flower* is *une fleur*

☐ **Now cover up the answers below and translate the following:**

☐ *(You can write your answers in)*

1. He has a dog and he wants a tree.

2. A goat is black but a fruit is red.

3. A fish eats a wasp.

4. The window is blue but the grass is green.

5. An insect is small but a fly is big.

_____

_____

_____

_____

_____

_____

_____

☐ *The answers are:*

1. Il a un chien et il veut un arbre.

2. Une chèvre est noire mais un fruit est rouge.

3. Un poisson mange une guêpe.

4. La fenêtre est bleue mais l'herbe est verte.

5. Un insecte est petit mais une mouche est grande.

Now cover up the answers below and translate the following:

☐ *(You can write your answers in)*

1. Une vache est petite et un insecte est grand.

2. Il est grand et elle est petite.

3. Il mange un canard bleu, mais elle mange une oie rouge.

4. Il voit une table rose, ou une table verte.

5. Elle a un rideau bleu et un placard blanc.

_____

_____

_____

_____

_____

_____

_____

_____

☐ *The answers are:*

1. A cow is small and an insect is big.
2. He is big and she is small.
3. He eats a blue duck, but she eats a red goose.
4. He sees a pink table, or a green table.
5. She has a blue curtain and a white cupboard.

TIME

□ **Think of each image in your mind's eye for about ten seconds**

- The French for **time** is **temps.** (TOn)
  Imagine keeping time with your **tongue.**

- The French for **second** is **seconde.** (SeGOHnD)
  Imagine seeing the Eiffel Tower for a split **second.**

- The French for **minute** is **minute.** (MEENooT)
  Imagine it takes you exactly one **minute** to run to the top of the Eiffel Tower.

- The French for **hour** is **heure.** (eR)
  Imagine you meet **her** every hour.

- The French for **day** is **jour.** (JOOR)
  Imagine not being **sure** what day it is.

- The French for **week** is **semaine.** (SeMEN)
  Imagine getting a **sermon** from your parents once a week.

- The French for **month** is **mois.** (MWA)
  Imagine your **ma** gives you pocket money once a month.

- The French for **year** is **an.** (On)
  Imagine thinking, "**Ah!** What a year!"

- The French for **morning** is **matin.** (MATAHn)
  Imagine going to a theater **matinee** in the morning.

- The French for **night** is **nuit.** (NWEE)
  Imagine thinking, "It would be night whe**n we** arrived home."

☐ *You can write your answers in*

- What is the English for **nuit**? (NWEE) _____

- What is the English for **matin**? (MATAHn) _____

- What is the English for **an**? (On) _____

- What is the English for **mois**? (MWA) _____

- What is the English for **semaine**? (SeMEN) _____

- What is the English for **jour**? (JOOR) _____

- What is the English for **heure**? (eR) _____

- What is the English for **minute**?
  (MEENooT) _____

- What is the English for **seconde**?
  (SeGOHnD) _____

- What is the English for **temps**? (TOn) _____

← *Look back for the answers*

☐ **Think of each image in your mind's eye for about ten seconds**

- The gender of **time** is *masculine*.   **le temps**
  Imagine a boxer looking anxiously at the time
  to see when his fight starts.

- The gender of **second** is *feminine*.   **la seconde**
  Imagine squirting perfume in short bursts of one
  second each.

- The gender of **minute** is *feminine*.   **la minute**
  Imagine bottles of perfume being sold from a
  shop counter at a rate of one a minute.

- The gender of **hour** is *feminine*.   **l'heure**
  Imagine lying in a bath of perfume for one
  hour.

- The gender of **day** is *masculine*.   **le jour**
  Imagine a boxer who has a fight a day.

- The gender of **week** is *feminine*.   **la semaine**
  Imagine giving a bottle of perfume to your
  mother once a week as a present.

- The gender of **month** is *masculine*.   **le mois**
  Imagine a boxer knocked out for a month.

- The gender of **year** is *masculine*.   **l'an**
  Imagine a boxer defending his title once a year.

- The gender of **morning** is *masculine*.   **le matin**
  Imagine a boxer getting up early in the morning
  to do his training.

- The gender of **night** is *feminine*.   **la nuit**
  Imagine a beautiful still night filled with
  fragrant perfume.

☐ *You can write your answers in*

- What is the gender and French for **night**? _____

- What is the gender and French for **morning**? _____

- What is the gender and French for **year**? _____

- What is the gender and French for **month**? _____

- What is the gender and French for **week**? _____

- What is the gender and French for **day**? _____

- What is the gender and French for **hour**? _____

- What is the gender and French for **minute**? _____

- What is the gender and French for **second**? _____

- What is the gender and French for **time**? _____

← *Look back for the answers*

ELEMENTARY GRAMMAR

In French, you normally make a word plural by adding an *s* at the end, but usually the *s* is not pronounced.

For example, *skirt* (*jupe*) becomes *skirts* (*jupes*) and both are pronounced in the same way (pronounced just as the word *jupe*).

The word for *the* in the plural is *les*—for both masculine and feminine words.

➜ *So,*

- *the skirts*   is *les jupes*

- *the dogs*   is *les chiens*

- *the black dogs* is *les chiens noirs*

Note that you normally also add an *s* to the end of the adjective, but this is not pronounced either.

Please note that if you have a masculine and a feminine noun together like

- *the dog and the cow are small*

then *small* is in a masculine form—i.e., *petits*.

The French for *are* in the sentence *The dog and the cat **are** black* is *sont* (pronounced SOHn).

➜ *So,*

- *The dog and the cat are black* is *Le chien et le chat sont noirs*

☐ **Now cover up the answers below and translate the following:**

☐ *(You can write your answers in)*

1. The grass and the tree are green.

2. The month and the year are quiet.

3. The hen and wasp are quick but quiet.

4. The insect and the fly are dirty and big.

5. The underpants and the sock are red and green.

_____

_____

_____

_____

_____

_____

_____

☐ *The answers are:*

1. L'herbe et l'arbre sont verts.
2. Le mois et l'an sont tranquilles.
3. La poule et la guêpe sont rapides mais tranquilles.
4. L'insecte et la mouche sont sales et grands.
5. Le slip et la chaussette sont rouges et verts.

□ **Now cover up the answers below and translate the following:**

□ *(You can write your answers in)*

1. Le chien et le fruit sont noirs.

2. L'heure et le jour sont tranquilles et gris.

3. Le matin et la nuit sont noirs.

4. La semaine est tranquille, et la seconde et la minute sont tranquilles.

5. Une fleur et un toit sont verts.

_____

_____

_____

_____

_____

_____

_____

□ *The answers are:*

1. The dog and the fruit are black.

2. The hour and the day are quiet and gray.

3. The morning and the night are black.

4. The week is quiet, and the second and the minute are quiet.

5. A flower and a roof are green.

☐ **Now cover up the answers below and translate the following:**

☐ *(You can write your answers in)*

1. The flowers and the wasps are small.

2. The dirty socks and the trousers are pretty.

3. The black shoes and the green pullovers are empty.

4. The hats and the jackets are heavy and red.

5. The cold kitchen and the big garden are empty and ugly.

_____

_____

_____

_____

_____

_____

_____

☐ *The answers are:*

1. Les fleurs et les guêpes sont petites.

2. Les chaussettes sales et le pantalon sont jolis.

3. Les chaussures noires et les pullovers verts sont vides.

4. Les chapeaux et les vestes sont lourds et rouges.
   (Note: A few words end with an *x*, not an *s*, in the plural.)

5. La cuisine froide et le grand jardin sont vides et laids.

Now cover up the answers below and translate the following:

    ☐ *(You can write your answers in)*

1. Les lapins et les chats sont petits.

2. Les vaches ou les truites sont grandes.

3. Les tables et les chiens sont lourds.

4. Les armoires et les chaises sont blanches.

5. Les chapeaux et les robes sont jolis mais lourds.

_____

_____

_____

_____

_____

_____

_____

_____

☐ *The answers are:*

1. The rabbits and the cats are small.

2. The cows or the trout are big.

3. The tables and the dogs are heavy.

4. The wardrobes and the chairs are white.

5. The hats and the dresses are pretty but heavy.

NUMBERS

☐ **Think of each image in your mind's eye for about ten seconds**

- The French for **one** is **un**. (en)
  Imagine eating one **on**ion.

- The French for **two** is **deux**. (De)
  Imagine thinking "two will **do**."

- The French for **three** is **trois**. (TRWA)
  Imagine you **try** to say trois three times.

- The French for **four** is **quatre**. (KATR)
  Imagine looking at four **cats.**

- The French for **five** is **cinq**. (SAHnK)
  Imagine watching as five ships **sank.**

- The French for **six** is **six**. (SEES)
  Imagine telling someone to **cease** saying, "six times six."

- The French for **seven** is **sept**. (SET)
  Imagine you **set** your alarm for seven o'clock.

- The French for **eight** is **huit**. (WEET)
  Imagine eight sheaves of **wheat.**

- The French for **nine** is **neuf**. (NeF)
  Imagine saying, "**Enough** is enough. A cat has nine lives."

- The French for **zero** is **zéro**. (ZAYROH)
  Imagine meeting someone at the Eiffel Tower at **zero** hour.

Please note: Numbers do not vary their endings, so they do not add an *s* in the plural.

- What is the English for **zéro**? (ZAYROH)   _____

- What is the English for **neuf**? (NeF)   _____

- What is the English for **huit**? (WEET)   _____

- What is the English for **sept**? (SET)   _____

- What is the English for **six**? (SEES)   _____

- What is the English for **cinq**? (SAHnK)   _____

- What is the English for **quatre**? (KATR)   _____

- What is the English for **trois**? (TRWA)   _____

- What is the English for **deux**? (De)   _____

- What is the English for **un**? (en)   _____

← *Look back for the answers*

☐ *You can write your answers in*

- What is the French for **zero**? _____

- What is the French for **nine**? _____

- What is the French for **eight**? _____

- What is the French for **seven**? _____

- What is the French for **six**? _____

- What is the French for **five**? _____

- What is the French for **four**? _____

- What is the French for **three**? _____

- What is the French for **two**? _____

- What is the French for **one**? _____

← *Look back for the answers*

☐ **Now cover up the answers below and translate the following:**

☐ *(You can write your answers in)*

1. Two flowers are red.

2. Four rabbits are thin.

3. Five insects and three flies are pretty.

4. Seven trees and nine dresses are heavy.

5. Eight skirts are white and three dresses are green.

_____

_____

_____

_____

_____

_____

_____

_____

☐ *The answers are:*

1. Deux fleurs sont rouges.

2. Quatre lapins sont minces.

3. Cinq insectes et trois mouches sont jolis.

4. Sept arbres et neuf robes sont lourds.

5. Huit jupes sont blanches et trois robes sont vertes.

84

☐ **Now cover up the answers below and translate the following:**

☐ *(You can write your answers in)*

1. Deux pullovers sont laids.

2. Quatre poissons sont blancs.

3. Six fils et sept filles sont sales.

4. Neuf mouches et huit guêpes sont noires.

5. Trois fleurs et sept murs sont rouges.

_____

_____

_____

_____

_____

_____

_____

☐ *The answers are:*

1. Two pullovers are ugly.
2. Four fish are white.
3. Six sons and seven daughters are dirty.
4. Nine flies and eight wasps are black.
5. Three flowers and seven walls are red.

SECTION 5

IN A RESTAURANT, TELLING TIME

IN THE RESTAURANT

☐ **Think of each image in your mind's eye for about ten seconds**

- The French for **restaurant** is **restaurant.**　　(RESTOROn)
  Imagine a **restaurant** at the top of the Eiffel Tower.

- The French for **knife** is **couteau.**　　(KOOTOH)
  Imagine someone who tries to **cut you** with a knife.

- The French for **fork** is **fourchette.**　　(FOORSHET)
  Imagine taking a fork and trying to **force it**
  through a door.

- The French for **spoon** is **cuiller.**　　(KWEE ER)
  Imagine a **queer**-shaped spoon.

- The French for **menu** is **carte.**　　(KART)
  Imagine a **cart** loaded to the top with menus.

- The French for **bill** is **addition.**　　(ADEESEE OHn)
  Imagine practicing your **addition** as you
  add up a bill.

- The French for **waiter** is **garçon.**　　(GARSOHn)
  Imagine a waiter who has left the **gas on** and
  burnt your meal.
  (Note: *Garçon* is the same as the word for *boy.*)

- The French for **waitress** is **serveuse.**　　(SERVeZ)
  Imagine demanding that the waitress gives you
  service.

- The French for **cup** is **tasse.**　　(TAS)
  Imagine a **tassel** hanging from the handle of a cup.

- The French for **plate** is **assiette.**　　(ASEE ET)
  Imagine looking for a plate and saying
  "I see it."

- What is the English for **assiette**?
  (ASEE ET)   _____

- What is the English for **tasse**? (TAS)   _____

- What is the English for **serveuse**?
  (SERVeZ)   _____

- What is the English for **garçon**?
  (GARSOHn)   _____

- What is the English for **addition**?
  (ADEESEE OHn)   _____

- What is the English for **carte**? (KART)   _____

- What is the English for **cuiller**?
  (KWEE ER)   _____

- What is the English for **fourchette**?
  (FOORSHET)   _____

- What is the English for **couteau**?
  (KOOTOH)   _____

- What is the English for **restaurant**?
  (RESTOROn)   _____

← *Look back for the answers*

☐ **Think of each image in your mind's eye for about ten seconds**

- The gender of **restaurant** is *masculine*.
  Imagine a boxer eating in a fashionable
  restaurant after a fight.

  le restaurant

- The gender of **knife** is *masculine*.
  Imagine a boxer stabbing his opponent with a
  knife.

  le couteau

- The gender of **fork** is *feminine*.
  Imagine stirring some perfume with a fork.

  la fourchette

- The gender of **spoon** is *feminine*.
  Imagine pouring perfume onto a teaspoon and
  then putting it onto yourself.

  la cuiller

- The gender of **menu** is *feminine*.
  Imagine a menu that smells of perfume when
  you sniff it.

  la carte

- The gender of **bill** is *feminine*.
  Imagine being presented with a bottle of
  perfume when your bill comes.

  l'addition

- The gender of **waiter** is *masculine*.
  Imagine a waiter serving you with boxing
  gloves on.

  le garçon

- The gender of **waitress** is *feminine*.
  Imagine a waitress smelling of cheap perfume.

  la serveuse

- The gender of **cup** is *feminine*.
  Imagine a cup full of perfume.

  la tasse

- The gender of **plate** is *feminine*.
  Imagine pouring some perfume onto a plate.

  l'assiette

☐ *You can write your answers in*

- What is the gender and French for **plate**?   _____

- What is the gender and French for **cup**?   _____

- What is the gender and French for **waitress**?   _____

- What is the gender and French for **waiter**?   _____

- What is the gender and French for **bill**?   _____

- What is the gender and French for **menu**?   _____

- What is the gender and French for **spoon**?   _____

- What is the gender and French for **fork**?   _____

- What is the gender and French for **knife**?   _____

- What is the gender and French for **restaurant**?   _____

← *Look back for the answers*

90

ELEMENTARY GRAMMAR

When you want to say *the dogs eat* or *the cats eat,* etc., then the word for *eat* is *mangent.* However, it sounds exactly like *mange* (MOnJ).

This is also true of the word *see—voient,* which sounds the same as *voit* (VWA).

➜ *So,*

- *the dogs see* is *les chiens voient* (pronounced VWA).

The word *have* in *the dogs have* is *ont* (pronounced OHn).

The word *want* in *the dogs want* is *veulent* (pronounced VeL).

➜ *So,*

- *the dog wants*   is *le chien veut*

- *the dogs and the cats want* is *les chiens et les chats veulent* (VeL)

➜ *So,*

- *the dogs want* is *les chiens veulent* (VeL)

- *the dogs see*   is *les chiens voient* (VWA)

- *the dogs eat*   is *les chiens mangent* (MOnJ)

- *the dogs have* is *les chiens ont* (OHn)

□ *(You can write your answers in)*

1. The heavy forks and the gold(en) knives are dirty.

2. The waiters want the little cup.

3. The waitresses eat the green grass.

4. The boys have the blue plates.

5. The mice and the geese see the big restaurant.

_____

_____

_____

_____

_____

_____

_____

_____

□ *The answers are:*

1. Les fourchettes lourdes et les couteaux dorés sont sales.

2. Les garçons veulent la petite tasse.

3. Les serveuses mangent l'herbe verte.

4. Les garçons ont les assiettes bleues.

5. Les souris et les oies voient le grand restaurant.

☐ *(You can write your answers in)*

1. Le garçon doré et la serveuse sale mangent cinq poules.

2. Les assiettes jaunes ont une tasse rouge.

3. Le père et la mère veulent l'addition.

4. Les cuillers voient les restaurants verts.

5. Il mange la carte mais les lapins mangent les fourchettes, et les tasses, et les assiettes.

_____

_____

_____

_____

_____

_____

☐ *The answers are:*

1. The gold(en) waiter and the dirty waitress eat five hens.

2. The yellow plates have a red cup.

3. The father and the mother want the bill.

4. The spoons see the green restaurants.

5. He eats the menu but the rabbits eat the forks, and the cups, and the plates.

SOME MORE RESTAURANT WORDS

☐ **Think of each image in your mind's eye for about ten seconds**

- The French for **cutlery** is **couvert.** (KOOVER)
  Imagine that you **cover** up the cutlery.

- The French for **tablecloth** is **nappe.** (NAP)
  Imagine taking a **nap** on a tablecloth.

- The French for **glass** is **verre.** (VER)
  Imagine telling the waiter that it is not **fair** that
  you don't have a glass.

- The French for **drink** is **boisson.** (BWASOHn)
  Imagine asking if you can talk to the **boss on**
  whether you can have free drinks in the cafeteria.

- The French for **food** is **nourriture.** (NOOREETooR)
  Imagine asking the waiter if there is food to
  nourish your body.

- The French for **lunch** is **déjeuner.** (DAYJeNAY)
  Imagine asking yourself if this is one of the
  days you may eat lunch.

- The French for **dinner** is **dîner.** (DEENAY)
  Imagine having **dinner** in the Eiffel Tower.

- The French for **meat** is **viande.** (VEE OnD)
  Imagine a German waiter saying, "**Ve hand** the
  meat to you."

- The French for **vegetable** is **légume.** (LAYGooM)
  Imagine you take gum out of your mouth when
  the vegetables are served, and **lay gum** all
  around the vegetables.

- The French for **tip** is **pourboire.** (POORBWAR)
  Imagine thinking, "This is a **poor bar.** I won't
  leave a tip."

- What is the English for **pourboire**?
  (POORBWAR)

  _____

- What is the English for **légume**?
  (LAYGooM)

  _____

- What is the English for **viande**?
  (VEE OnD)

  _____

- What is the English for **dîner**? (DEENAY)

  _____

- What is the English for **déjeuner**?
  (DAYJeNAY)

  _____

- What is the English for **nourriture**?
  (NOOREETooR)

  _____

- What is the English for **boisson**?
  (BWASOHn)

  _____

- What is the English for **verre**? (VER)

  _____

- What is the English for **nappe**? (NAP)

  _____

- What is the English for **couvert**?
  (KOOVER)

  _____

← *Look back for the answers*

☐ **Think of each image in your mind's eye for about ten seconds**

- The gender of **cutlery** is *masculine*.　　　　**le couvert**
  Imagine a boxer laying a table with cutlery.

- The gender of **tablecloth** is *feminine*.　　　　**la nappe**
  Imagine spraying perfume on a tablecloth to
  make it smell nice.

- The gender of **glass** is *masculine*.　　　　**le verre**
  Imagine a boxer drinking from a glass before he
  goes out to fight.

- The gender of **drink** is *feminine*.　　　　**la boisson**
  Imagine your drinks smell strongly of perfume.

- The gender of **food** is *feminine*.　　　　**la nourriture**
  Imagine someone spraying all your food with
  perfume before a meal.

- The gender of **lunch** is *masculine*.　　　　**le déjeuner**
  Imagine a boxer eating a light lunch before a
  fight.

- The gender of **dinner** is *masculine*.　　　　**le dîner**
  Imagine a boxer celebrating a victory with a big
  dinner in an expensive restaurant.

- The gender of **meat** is *feminine*.　　　　**la viande**
  Imagine marinating meat in perfume.

- The gender of **vegetable** is *masculine*.　　　　**le légume**
  Imagine a boxer eating a big plate of
  vegetables.

- The gender of **tip** is *masculine*.　　　　**le pourboire**
  Imagine a famous boxer leaving a miserly tip.

You can write your answers in

- What is the gender and French for **tip**? _____

- What is the gender and French for **vegetable**? _____

- What is the gender and French for **meat**? _____

- What is the gender and French for **dinner**? _____

- What is the gender and French for **lunch**? _____

- What is the gender and French for **food**? _____

- What is the gender and French for **drink**? _____

- What is the gender and French for **glass**? _____

- What is the gender and French for **tablecloth**? _____

- What is the gender and French for **cutlery**? _____

← *Look back for the answers*

ELEMENTARY GRAMMAR

When you ask questions in French, you can always do so by keeping the same word order as normal, but putting the words *est-ce que* first. (*Est-ce que* is pronounced ESKe.) Imagine you *ask a* question.

➜ *So,*

- *The dogs are black* is *Les chiens sont noirs*

- *Are the dogs black?* is *Est-ce que les chiens sont noirs?*

- *The restaurant is dirty* is *Le restaurant est sale*

- *Is the restaurant dirty?* is *Est-ce que le restaurant est sale?*

However, if the word that follows *est-ce que* begins with a vowel, then the *e* of *que* is dropped.

➜ *For example,*

- *He is ugly* is *Il est laid*

- *Is he ugly?* is *Est-ce qu'il est laid?*

Now cover up the answers below and translate the following:

☐ *(You can write your answers in)*

1. Does he eat the tired fish or the food?

2. Does she have the drinks?

3. Do the thin dogs and the big cats eat the tablecloth, or the menu?

4. Do the seven flies want a yellow glass?

5. Does the little waiter want a big tip?

_____

_____

_____

_____

_____

_____

_____

☐ *The answers are:*

1. Est-ce qu'il mange le poisson fatigué ou la nourriture?

2. Est-ce qu'elle a les boissons?

3. Est-ce que les chiens minces et les grands chats mangent la nappe, ou la carte?

4. Est-ce que les sept mouches veulent un verre jaune?

5. Est-ce que le petit garçon veut un grand pourboire?

☐ **Now cover up the answers below and translate the following:**

☐ *(You can write your answers in)*

1. Est-ce que la viande est chaude?

2. Est-ce qu'il a le couvert?

3. Est-ce que les trois garçons voient les tables rouges?

4. Est-ce que les pourboires sont grands?

5. Est-ce que les légumes et les verres sont verts?

_____

_____

_____

_____

_____

_____

_____

☐ *The answers are:*

1. Is the meat hot?
2. Has he the cutlery?
3. Do the three boys see the red tables?
4. Are the tips big?
5. Are the vegetables and the glasses green?

TELLING TIME (1)

☐ **Think of each image in your mind's eye for about ten seconds**

In order to tell time in French, you will need to learn a few more words.

- The French for **ten** is **dix.**   (DEES)
  Imagine you **dis**miss ten soldiers.

- The French for **eleven** is **onze.**   (OHnZ)
  Imagine **on the** stroke of eleven, you shoot
  eleven football players.

- The French for **12 o'clock (noon, midday)**   (MEEDEE)
  is **midi.**
  Imagine meeting someone at **midday** at the
  Eiffel Tower.

- The French for **12 o'clock (midnight)** is **minuit.**   (MEENWEE)
  Imagine asking someone "Do you **mean we**
  should see you at midnight?"

- The French for **quarter** is **quart.**   (KAR)
  Imagine you cut a **car** in quarters.

- The French for **half** is **demie.**   (DeMEE)
  Imagine you saw a **dummy** in half.

- The French for **twenty** is **vingt.**   (VAHn)
  Imagine a twenty-year-old **van.**

- The French for **twenty-five** is **vingt-cinq.**   (VAHnT-SAHnK)
  Imagine your **van sank** into the river at
  twenty-five past the hour.

☐ *You can write your answers in*

- What is the English for **vingt-cinq**?
  (VAHnT-SAHnK)   _____

- What is the English for **vingt**? (VAHn)   _____

- What is the English for **demie**? (DeMEE)   _____

- What is the English for **quart**? (KAR)   _____

- What is the English for **minuit**?
  (MEENWEE)   _____

- What is the English for **midi**? (MEEDEE)   _____

- What is the English for **onze**? (OHnZ)   _____

- What is the English for **dix**? (DEES)   _____

← *Look back for the answers*

- What is the French for **twenty-five**?   _____

- What is the French for **twenty**?   _____

- What is the French for **half**?   _____

- What is the French for **quarter**?   _____

- What is the French for **12 o'clock midnight**?   _____

- What is the French for **12 o'clock noon**?   _____

- What is the French for **eleven**?   _____

- What is the French for **ten**?   _____

← *Look back for the answers*

ELEMENTARY GRAMMAR: TELLING TIME (2)

As you learned earlier, the French for *hour* is *heure,* which is feminine.

The French for *what?* in the feminine is *quelle* (pronounced KEL).
Imagine thinking, "What? *Kill* her!"

To say *What time is it?* you simply say *What hour is it?:*

- *Quelle heure est-il?* (pronounced KEL eR ET EEL)

To answer the question in French, for example, *It is one o'clock, it is two o'clock,* etc., the literal translation is *It is one hour, it is two hours,* and so on.

➡ *So,*

- *It is one o'clock* is *It is one hour*
                           Il est une heure

- *It is two o'clock* is *It is two hours*
                           Il est deux heures

➡ *And,*

- *It is twelve o'clock (noon)*   is *Il est midi*

- *It is twelve o'clock (midnight)* is *Il est minuit*

☐ **Now cover up the answers below and translate the following:**

☐ *(You can write your answers in)*

1. It is five o'clock.

2. It is six o'clock.

3. It is 12 o'clock (midnight).

4. It is ten o'clock.

5. It is seven o'clock.

_____

_____

_____

_____

_____

_____

_____

☐ *The answers are:*

1. Il est cinq heures.
2. Il est six heures.
3. Il est minuit.
4. Il est dix heures.
5. Il est sept heures.

TELLING TIME (3)

When you want to say *It is five after seven* or *ten after eight* or *twenty after nine,* etc., then you simply put the number of minutes after the hour.

➜ *For example,*

- *seven hours five* is *five after seven*
  sept heures cinq

- *ten hours ten* is *ten after ten*
  dix heures dix

So, to say *It is five after eleven,* you just say *Il est onze heures cinq.*

To say, *It is quarter after* or *half past the hour,* you simply say, for example, *seven hours and quarter* or *seven hours and half.*

➜ *So,*

- *quarter after three* is *trois heures et quart*

- *half past five* is *cinq heures et demie*

108

☐ **Now cover up the answers below and translate the following:**

☐ *(You can write your answers in)*

1. It is quarter after five.

2. It is twenty-five after three.

3. It is five after one.

4. It is ten after nine.

5. It is twenty after eight.

_____

_____

_____

_____

_____

_____

_____

☐ *The answers are:*

1. Il est cinq heures et quart.
2. Il est trois heures vingt-cinq.
3. Il est une heure cinq.
4. Il est neuf heures dix.
5. Il est huit heures vingt.

TELLING TIME (4)

If you want to say *It is five to six,* and so on, then in French you say:

- *It is six hours minus five*

The French for *minus* (or *less*) is *moins* (pronounced MWAHn). Imagine you *moan* for less.

➔ *So,*

- *It is five to seven* is *It is seven hours minus five*
  Il est sept heures moins cinq

- *It is twenty to nine* is *It is nine hours minus twenty*
  Il est neuf heures moins vingt

There is one final point:

When you want to say *It is quarter to ten* or *quarter to eleven,* etc., the *quarter* is *le quart.*

➔ *So,*

- *It is quarter to four* is *Il est quatre heures moins le quart*

☐ **Now cover up the answers below and translate the following:**

☐ *(You can write your answers in)*

1. It is quarter to six.

2. It is half past four.

3. It is twenty to midnight.

4. It is twenty-five after four.

5. It is five to one.

_____

_____

_____

_____

_____

_____

_____

_____

☐ *The answers are:*

1. Il est six heures moins le quart.

2. Il est quatre heures et demie.

3. Il est minuit moins vingt.

4. Il est quatre heures vingt-cinq.

5. Il est une heure moins cinq.

☐ **Now cover up the answers below and translate the following:**

    ☐ *(You can write your answers in)*

1. Il est cinq heures moins le quart.

2. Il est sept heures et demie.

3. Il est trois heures vingt.

4. Il est minuit.

5. Il est onze heures moins dix.

_____

_____

_____

_____

_____

_____

_____

_____

☐ *The answers are:*

1. It is quarter to five.
2. It is half past seven.
3. It is twenty after three.
4. It is midnight.
5. It is ten to eleven.

SECTION 6

FOOD AND DRINK

SOME FOOD AND DRINK WORDS

☐ **Think of each image in your mind's eye for about ten seconds**

- The French for **cabbage** is **chou.**   (SHOO)
  Imagine a cabbage growing out of a **shoe.**

- The French for **lettuce** is **laitue.**   (LAYToo)
  Imagine thinking that it is too **late to** eat
  lettuce.

- The French for **bean** is **haricot.**   (AREEKOH)
  Imagine eating **haricot** beans.

- The French for **potato** is **pomme de terre.**   (POM De TER)
  Imagine you throw potatoes at terrorists
  carrying bombs: potatoes are **bomb deter**rents.

- The French for **tomato** is **tomate.**   (TOMAT)
  Imagine throwing **tomatoes** at the Eiffel Tower.

- The French for **egg** is **oeuf.**   (eF)
  Imagine telling a chicken to get **off** her egg.

- The French for **butter** is **beurre.**   (BeR)
  Imagine you hear a cat **purr** after it has eaten
  some butter.

- The French for **bread** is **pain.**   (PAHn)
  Imagine putting loaves of bread in a **pan.**

- The French for **milk** is **lait.**   (LAY)
  Imagine a hen which **lays** a bottle of milk.

- The French for **water** is **eau.**   (OH)
  Imagine that you **owe** a miserly Frenchman for
  a glass of water.

113

You can write your answers in

- What is the English for **eau**? (OH) _____

- What is the English for **lait**? (LAY) _____

- What is the English for **pain**? (PAHn) _____

- What is the English for **beurre**? (BeR) _____

- What is the English for **oeuf**? (eF) _____

- What is the English for **tomate**? (TOMAT) _____

- What is the English for **pomme de terre**? _____
  (POM De TER)

- What is the English for **haricot**? _____
  (AREEKOH)

- What is the English for **laitue**? (LAYToo) _____

- What is the English for **chou**? (SHOO)

← *Look back for the answers*

□ **Think of each image in your mind's eye for about ten seconds**

- The gender of **cabbage** is *masculine*.   **le chou**
  Imagine a boxer eating a cabbage.

- The gender of **lettuce** is *feminine*.   **la laitue**
  Imagine using perfume as a lettuce dressing—
  it tastes awful!

- The gender of **bean** is *masculine*.   **le haricot**
  Imagine a boxer eating baked beans.

- The gender of **potato** is *feminine*.   **la pomme de terre**
  Imagine covering your potatoes with a
  perfume instead of salt.

- The gender of **tomato** is *feminine*.   **la tomate**
  Imagine crushing tomatoes to make tomato
  perfume.

- The gender of **egg** is *masculine*.   **l'oeuf**
  Imagine a boxer filling himself with raw eggs to
  make himself stronger.

- The gender of **butter** is *masculine*.   **le beurre**
  Imagine a boxer smearing himself with butter to
  make himself more difficult to hit.

- The gender of **bread** is *masculine*.   **le pain**
  Imagine a boxer stuffing himself with bread to
  make himself heavier.

- The gender of **milk** is *masculine*.   **le lait**
  Imagine a boxer drinking pints of milk to make
  himself stronger.

- The gender of **water** is *feminine*.   **l'eau**
  Imagine the perfume "Eau-de-Cologne."

You can write your answers in

- What is the gender and French for **water**?   _____

- What is the gender and French for **milk**?   _____

- What is the gender and French for **bread**?   _____

- What is the gender and French for **butter**?   _____

- What is the gender and French for **egg**?   _____

- What is the gender and French for **tomato**?   _____

- What is the gender and French for **potato**?   _____

- What is the gender and French for **bean**?   _____

- What is the gender and French for **lettuce**?   _____

- What is the gender and French for **cabbage**?   _____

← *Look back for the answers*

ELEMENTARY GRAMMAR

The French word for *yes* is *oui* (WEE). Imagine thinking "Yes, *we* want it."

The French word for *no* is *non* (NOHn). Imagine thinking "No! *No!*"

When you want to say *not* in French, for example, *she does not eat,* then you must say *she eats not.*

The word for *not* is *pas* (PA). Imagine thinking "Not my *pa* again drunk."

However, you must also add the word *ne* (pronounced Ne).

➜ *So,*

- *She eats not (she does not eat)* is *elle ne mange pas*

➜ *For example,*

- *He does not want the cabbage* is *He wants not the cabbage:
  Il ne veut pas le chou*

- *The dog does not eat the cat* is *The dog eats not the cat:
  Le chien ne mange pas le chat*

There is one final point:

If the *ne* comes before a word that starts with a vowel (for example, *est*), then *ne* becomes *n'*.

➜ *So,*

- *Il ne mange pas* is *He does not eat*

but

- *He is not big* is *Il n'est pas grand*

117

☐ **Now cover up the answers below and translate the following:**

☐ *(You can write your answers in)*

1. The green cabbage is not dirty.

2. The big potatoes are not black.

3. The quiet tomato does not see the blue beans.

4. The gray egg and the orange butter do not want the green bread.

5. The cold milk and the hot water are not heavy.

_____

_____

_____

_____

_____

_____

_____

_____

☐ *The answers are:*

1. Le chou vert n'est pas sale.

2. Les grandes pommes de terre ne sont pas noires.

3. La tomate tranquille ne voit pas les haricots bleus.

4. L'oeuf gris et le beurre orange ne veulent pas le pain vert.

5. Le lait froid et l'eau chaude ne sont pas lourds.

☐ **Now cover up the answers below and translate the following:**

☐ *(You can write your answers in)*

1. Oui, il n'est pas rouge.

2. Non, elle ne mange pas le lapin.

3. Non, il ne voit pas le chou.

4. Les tomates et les pommes de terre ne sont pas sales.

5. Le frère n'a pas les petits haricots.

_____

_____

_____

_____

_____

_____

_____

_____

☐ *The answers are:*

1. Yes, he is not red.

2. No, she does not eat the rabbit.

3. No, he does not see the cabbage.

4. The tomatoes and the potatoes are not dirty.

5. The brother does not have the little beans.

MORE FOOD AND DRINK WORDS

☐ **Think of each image in your mind's eye for about ten seconds**

- The French for **beer** is **bière.** (BEE ER)
  Imagine pouring **beer** from the top of the Eiffel
  Tower.

- The French for **wine** is **vin.** (VAHn)
  Imagine a **van** delivering bottles of wine.

- The French for **apple** is **pomme.** (POM)
  Imagine someone who has an apple on his or
  her head instead of a **pom-pom.**

- The French for **pear** is **poire.** (PWAR)
  Imagine being so **poor** you can only afford
  cheap pears.

- The French for **peach** is **pêche.** (PESH)
  Imagine a child being a **pest** until you give him
  a peach.

- The French for **coffee** is **café.** (KAFAY)
  Imagine drinking coffee in a French **café.**

- The French for **cheese** is **fromage.** (FROMAJ)
  Imagine someone who can't tell cheese **from
  marg**arine.

- The French for **mushroom** is **champignon.** (SHOnPEENYOHn)
  Imagine you have raised a **champion**
  mushroom.

- The French for **garlic** is **ail.** (A EE)
  Imagine someone poking you in the **eye** with a
  piece of garlic.

- The French for **snail** is **escargot.** (ESKARGOH)
  Imagine a ship with **its cargo** of snails.

- What is the English for **escargot**? (ESKARGOH) _____

- What is the English for **ail**? (A EE) _____

- What is the English for **champignon**? (SHOnPEENYOHn) _____

- What is the English for **fromage**? (FROMAJ) _____

- What is the English for **café**? (KAFAY) _____

- What is the English for **pêche**? (PESH) _____

- What is the English for **poire**? (PWAR) _____

- What is the English for **pomme**? (POM) _____

- What is the English for **vin**? (VAHn) _____

- What is the English for **bière**? (BEE ER) _____

← *Look back for the answers*

☐ **Think of each image in your mind's eye for about ten seconds**

- The gender of **beer** is *feminine.*   **la bière**
  Imagine your beer tasting like perfume—you
  spit it out.

- The gender of **wine** is *masculine.*   **le vin**
  Imagine a boxer drinking a whole bottle of wine
  before a fight.

- The gender of **apple** is *feminine.*   **la pomme**
  Imagine marinating apples in a perfume sauce.

- The gender of **pear** is *feminine.*   **la poire**
  Imagine a perfume that smells of pears.

- The gender of **peach** is *feminine.*   **la pêche**
  Imagine using peach brandy as perfume.

- The gender of **coffee** is *masculine.*   **le café**
  Imagine boxers drinking coffee after a fight.

- The gender of **cheese** is *masculine.*   **le fromage**
  Imagine a boxer filling his gloves with cheese to
  make the boxing gloves heavier.

- The gender of **mushroom** is *masculine.*   **le champignon**
  Imagine a boxer eating a magic mushroom to
  make him box better.

- The gender of **garlic** is *masculine.*   **l'ail**
  Imagine a boxer breathing garlic at his opponent
  to put him off his boxing.

- The gender of **snail** is *masculine.*   **l'escargot**
  Imagine a snail crawling up a boxer's leg during
  a fight.

☐ *You can write your answers in*

- What is the gender and French for **snail**?   _____

- What is the gender and French for **garlic**?   _____

- What is the gender and French for
  mushroom?   _____

- What is the gender and French for **cheese**?   _____

- What is the gender and French for **coffee**?   _____

- What is the gender and French for **peach**?   _____

- What is the gender and French for **pear**?   _____

- What is the gender and French for **apple**?   _____

- What is the gender and French for **wine**?   _____

- What is the gender and French for **beer**?   _____

← *Look back for the answers*

SOME MORE USEFUL WORDS

☐ **Think of each image in your mind's eye for about ten seconds**

- The French for **very** is **très**.   (TRAY)
  Imagine a **tray** very full.

- The French for **soon** is **bientôt**.   (BEE AHnTOH)
  Imagine thinking "I will have **been to** that
  place soon."

- The French for **here** is **ici**.   (EESEE)
  Imagine thinking "It is very **easy** here to learn
  French."

- The French for **there** is **là**.   (LA)
  Imagine thinking, "Ooh **la** la! There's a gift for
  me."

- The French for **quite** is **assez**.   (ASAY)
  Imagine thinking "**I say,** he is quite clever."

- The French for **easy** is **facile**.   (FASEEL)
  Imagine thinking "He has an easy but **facile**
  manner."

- The French for **difficult** is **difficile**.   (DEEFEESEEL)
  Imagine it is **difficult** to climb the Eiffel Tower.

- The French for **high** is **haut**.   (OH)
  Imagine thinking "**Oh,** I am very high up."

- The French for **angry** is **fâché**.   (FASHAY)
  Imagine a very angry **fascist**.

- The French for **good** is **bon**.   (BOHn)
  Imagine eating good **bon**bons—bonbons are
  goody goodies.

- What is the English for **bon**? (BOHn) ⎯⎯⎯⎯⎯

- What is the English for **fâché**? (FASHAY) ⎯⎯⎯⎯⎯

- What is the English for **haut**? (OH) ⎯⎯⎯⎯⎯

- What is the English for **difficile**? (DEEFEESEEL) ⎯⎯⎯⎯⎯

- What is the English for **facile**? (FASEEL) ⎯⎯⎯⎯⎯

- What is the English for **assez**? (ASAY) ⎯⎯⎯⎯⎯

- What is the English for **là**? (LA) ⎯⎯⎯⎯⎯

- What is the English for **ici**? (EESEE) ⎯⎯⎯⎯⎯

- What is the English for **bientôt**? (BEE AHnTOH) ⎯⎯⎯⎯⎯

- What is the English for **très**? (TRAY) ⎯⎯⎯⎯⎯

← *Look back for the answers*

☐ *You can write your answers in*

- What is the French for **very**? _____

- What is the French for **soon**? _____

- What is the French for **here**? _____

- What is the French for **there**? _____

- What is the French for **quite**? _____

- What is the French for **easy**? _____

- What is the French for **difficult**? _____

- What is the French for **high**? _____

- What is the French for **angry**? _____

- What is the French for **good**? _____

← *Look back for the answers*

ELEMENTARY GRAMMAR: WAS AND WERE

The French for the words *was* and *were* are pronounced AYTAY, although they are spelled differently.

- *était*   is *was*

- *étaient* is *were*

Imagine wishing *I was eighty* again.

➜   *So,*

- *The dog was blue*   is *Le chien était bleu*

- *The dogs were blue* is *Les chiens étaient bleus*

I was is *j'étais* (pronounced JAYTAY).

☐ **Now cover up the answers below and translate the following:**

☐ *(You can write your answers in)*

1. The cold beer was very good.

2. The apples and the pears were not very red.

3. The black coffee and the white cheese see a very big restaurant.

4. The snails do not eat a thin mushroom.

5. The lunch and the dinner were quite good, but the vegetables are not very hot.

_____

_____

_____

_____

_____

_____

☐ *The answers are:*

1. La bière froide était très bonne.

2. Les pommes et les poires n'étaient pas très rouges.

3. Le café noir et le fromage blanc voient un très grand restaurant.

4: Les escargots ne mangent pas un champignon mince.

5. Le déjeuner et le dîner étaient assez bons, mais les légumes ne sont pas très chauds.

☐ **Now cover up the answers below and translate the following:**

☐ *(You can write your answers in)*

1. Le vin n'était pas ici.

2. Les pêches et l'ail étaient très bons.

3. Le mari était assez fâché, mais la femme était très tranquille.

4. Les garçons étaient très difficiles, mais les serveuses étaient très bonnes.

5. Le plafond était très haut.

_____

_____

_____

_____

_____

_____

☐ *The answers are:*

1. The wine was not here.

2. The peaches and the garlic were very good.

3. The husband was quite angry, but the wife was very quiet.

4. The waiters were very difficult, but the waitresses were very good.

5. The ceiling was very high.

SECTION 7

SHOPPING AND BUSINESS WORDS

BASIC SHOPPING AND BUSINESS WORDS

☐ **Think of each image in your mind's eye for about ten seconds**

- The French for **worker** is **ouvrier.** (OOVREE AY)
  Imagine a worker shouting at you "I'm **over here.**"

- The French for **company** (firm) is **compagnie.** (KOHnPANYEE)
  Imagine your **company** buying the Eiffel Tower.

- The French for **factory** is **usine.** (ooZEEN)
  Imagine asking "Have **you seen** the factory?"

- The French for **manager** is **directeur.** (DEEREKTeR)
  Imagine that when you ask to see the manager, the board of **directors** is brought to you.

- The French for **boss** is **patron.** (PATROHn)
  Imagine the boss of a business being very **patron**izing to you.

- The French for **office** is **bureau.** (BooROH)
  Imagine a writing **bureau** in an office.

- The French for **shop** is **magasin.** (MAGAZAHn)
  Imagine every shop you go into sells **magazines.**

- The French for **price** is **prix.** (PREE)
  Imagine asking the price of admission to see a Grand **Prix** race. (Note: *Prix* also means prize.)

- The French for **check** is **chèque.** (SHEK)
  Imagine paying by **check** to get into the Eiffel Tower.

- The French for **salary** is **salaire.** (SALER)
  Imagine being paid your **salary** at the top of the Eiffel Tower.

☐ *You can write your answers in*

- What is the English for **salaire**? (SALER) ———————————

- What is the English for **chèque**? (SHEK) ———————————

- What is the English for **prix**? (PREE) ———————————

- What is the English for **magasin**? ———————————
  (MAGAZAHn)

- What is the English for **bureau**? ———————————
  (BooROH)

- What is the English for **patron**? ———————————
  (PATROHn)

- What is the English for **directeur**? ———————————
  (DEEREKTeR)

- What is the English for **usine**? (ooZEEN) ———————————

- What is the English for **compagnie**? ———————————
  (KOHnPANYEE)

- What is the English for **ouvrier**? ———————————
  (OOVREE AY)

← *Look back for the answers*

☐ **Think of each image in your mind's eye for about ten seconds**

- The gender of **worker** is *masculine.*   **l'ouvrier**
  Imagine a worker getting ready for a boxing
  match.

- The gender of **company** (firm) is *feminine.*   **la compagnie**
  Imagine a company which makes perfume.

- The gender of **factory** is *feminine.*   **l'usine**
  Imagine a factory making perfume.

- The gender of **manager** is *masculine.*   **le directeur**
  Imagine a boxing manager.

- The gender of **boss** is *masculine.*   **le patron**
  Imagine the boss of a boxing school, smoking a
  fat cigar.

- The gender of **office** is *masculine.*   **le bureau**
  Imagine a boxer waiting in his manager's office.

- The gender of **shop** is *masculine.*   **le magasin**
  Imagine a boxer going wild in a shop, scattering
  all the goods.

- The gender of **price** is *masculine.*   **le prix**
  Imagine a boxer asking the price of goods.

- The gender of **check** is *masculine.*   **le chèque**
  Imagine a boxer being presented with a check
  after winning a fight.

- The gender of **salary** is *masculine.*   **le salaire**
  Imagine a boxer collecting a salary once a
  month, even though he does not fight.

☐ *You can write your answers in*

- What is the gender and French for **salary**? ————————

- What is the gender and French for **check**? ————————

- What is the gender and French for **price**? ————————

- What is the gender and French for **shop**? ————————

- What is the gender and French for **office**? ————————

- What is the gender and French for **boss**? ————————

- What is the gender and French for **manager**? ————————

- What is the gender and French for **factory**? ————————

- What is the gender and French for **company** (firm)? ————————

- What is the gender and French for **worker**? ————————

← *Look back for the answers*

SOME MORE USEFUL WORDS

☐ **Think of each image in your mind's eye for about ten seconds**

- The French for **where** is **où**.   (OO)
  Imagine thinking, "**Ooh! Where** are you?"

- The French for **why** is **pourquoi**.   (POORKWA)
  Imagine thinking, "**Why** is that **poor quack**ing
  duck ill?"

- The French for **how** is **comment**.   (KOMOn)
  Imagine saying, "**How** well you have **come on**."

- The French for **when** is **quand**.   (KOn)
  Imagine asking **when** the **con** man called.

- The French for **because** is **parce que**.   (PARS Ke)
  Imagine you get into your office **because** you
  have a **pass key**.

☐ *You can write your answers in*

- What is the English for **parce que**?   _____
  (PARS Ke)

- What is the English for **quand**? (KOn)   _____

- What is the English for **comment**?   _____
  (KOMOn)

- What is the English for **pourquoi**?   _____
  (POORKWA)

- What is the English for **où**? (OO)   _____

← *Look back for the answers*

☐ *You can write your answers in*

- What is the French for **because**? _____

- What is the French for **when**? _____

- What is the French for **how**? _____

- What is the French for **why**? _____

- What is the French for **where**? _____

← *Look back for the answers*

ELEMENTARY GRAMMAR

The words *where, why, when, how* are sometimes used with the word *est-ce que* when asking questions.

As you learned earlier, you use *est-ce que* when you want to turn a sentence that already exists into a question.

→ *For example,*

Is the worker blue? is a question, so you should put *est-ce que* in front:

- *Est-ce que l'ouvrier est bleu?*

- *Why is the worker blue?* is *Pourquoi est-ce que l'ouvrier est bleu?*

- *When is the roof dirty?* is *Quand est-ce que le toit est sale?*

→ *Here is another example:*

- *How does the boss want the fish?* is *Comment est-ce que le patron veut le poisson?*

However, if you just want to say *where is* or *where are*, you simply say:

où est or *où sont* without the *est-ce que*.

→ *So,*

- *Where is the boss?* is *Où est le patron?*

☐ **Now cover up the answers below and translate the following:**

☐ *(You can write your answers in)*

1. Where is the office?

2. Why is the shop quiet?

3. How does he eat the duck?

4. When are the factories quiet?

5. Where is the worker?

_____

_____

_____

_____

_____

_____

_____

☐ *The answers are:*

1. Où est le bureau?

2. Pourquoi est-ce que le magasin est tranquille?

3. Comment est-ce qu'il mange le canard?

4. Quand est-ce que les usines sont tranquilles?

5. Où est l'ouvrier?

☐ **Now cover up the answers below and translate the following:**

☐ *(You can write your answers in)*

1. Pourquoi est-ce que le directeur est fâché?

2. Où est le patron et où est la compagnie?

3. Comment est-ce que l'ouvrier voit le chèque?

4. Quand est-ce que le patron mange le salaire?

5. Où sont les prix et où sont les chèques?

_____

_____

_____

_____

_____

_____

_____

☐ *The answers are:*

1. Why is the manager angry?

2. Where is the boss and where is the company?

3. How does the worker see the check?

4. When does the boss eat the salary?

5. Where are the prices and where are the checks?

MORE SHOPPING AND BUSINESS WORDS

☐ **Think of each image in your mind's eye for about ten seconds**

- The French for **receipt** is **reçu.** (ReSoo)
  Imagine someone **rescuing** a receipt from you.

- The French for **mistake** is **erreur.** (EReR)
  Imagine being told that **errors** and mistakes
  cannot be rectified.

- The French for **vacation** is **vacances.** (VAKOnS)
  Imagine all the staff have gone on their
  vacation to the Eiffel Tower.

- The French for **cash register (cash till)** is **caisse.** (KES)
  Imagine putting a cash register in a **case.**

- The French for **goods** is **marchandise.** (MARSHOnDEEZ)
  Imagine selling goods and **merchandise.**

- The French for **accountant** is **comptable.** (KOHnTABL)
  Imagine thinking your accountant is
  contemptible.

- The French for **contract** is **contrat.** (KOHnTRA)
  Imagine signing a **contract** to buy the Eiffel
  Tower.

- The French for **striker** is **gréviste.** (GRAYVEEST)
  Imagine a **gray vest** on a striker outside a
  factory.

- The French for **salesman** is **vendeur.** (VOnDeR)
  Imagine a salesman trying to sell you a **van door.**

- The French for **secretary** is **secrétaire.** (SeKRAYTER)
  Imagine a pretty **secretary** jumping from the
  Eiffel Tower.

☐ *You can write your answers in*

- What is the English for **secrétaire**?   _____
  (SeKRAYTER)

- What is the English for **vendeur**?   _____
  (VOnDeR)

- What is the English for **gréviste**?   _____
  (GRAYVEEST)

- What is the English for **contrat**?   _____
  (KOHnTRA)

- What is the English for **comptable**?   _____
  (KOHnTABL)

- What is the English for **marchandise**?   _____
  (MARSHOnDEEZ)

- What is the English for **caisse**? (KES)   _____

- What is the English for **vacances**?   _____
  (VAKOnS)

- What is the English for **erreur**? (EReR)   _____

- What is the English for **reçu**? (ReSoo)   _____

← *Look back for the answers*

☐ **Think of each image in your mind's eye for about ten seconds**

- The gender of **receipt** is *masculine*.   **le reçu**
  Imagine a boxer asking for a receipt for his
  prize.

- The gender of **mistake** is *feminine*.   **l'erreur**
  Imagine putting on perfume by mistake.

- The gender of **vacation** is *feminine*.   **les vacances**
  Imagine bringing some bottles of perfume from
  your vacation.

- The gender of **cash register** is *feminine*.   **la caisse**
  Imagine a shop assistant ringing up a payment
  for perfume on a cash register.

- The gender of **goods** is *feminine*.   **la marchandise**
  Imagine buying goods that include boxes of
  perfume.

- The gender of **accountant** is *masculine*.   **le comptable**
  Imagine a boxer talking to his accountant about
  his tax problems.

- The gender of **contract** is *masculine*.   **le contrat**
  Imagine boxers going over a contract to fight.

- The gender of **striker** is *masculine*.   **le gréviste**
  Imagine two boxers striking each other.
  (But remember *striker* has a different meaning.)

- The gender of **salesman** is *masculine*.   **le vendeur**
  Imagine a salesman selling miniature boxers.

- The gender of **secretary** is *feminine*.   **la secrétaire**
  Imagine a secretary covering herself with
  perfume.

☐ *You can write your answers in*

- What is the gender and French for **secretary**? _____

- What is the gender and French for **salesman**? _____

- What is the gender and French for **striker**? _____

- What is the gender and French for **contract**? _____

- What is the gender and French for **accountant**? _____

- What is the gender and French for **goods**? _____

- What is the gender and French for **cash register**? _____

- What is the gender and French for **vacation**? _____

- What is the gender and French for **mistake**? _____

- What is the gender and French for **receipt**? _____

← *Look back for the answers*

ADJECTIVES

- The French for **young** is **jeune.**   (JeN)
  Imagine getting drunk on **gin** when you are
  young.

- The French for **clean** is **propre.**   (PROPR)
  Imagine looking clean and **proper.**

- The French for **hard** is **dur.**   (DooR)
  Imagine something hard and **dur**able.

- The French for **full** is **plein.**   (PLAHn)
  Imagine a full **plan** of action.

- The French for **dry** is **sec.**   (SEK)
  Imagine putting dry clothes in a **sack.**
  (Note: The feminine of *sec* is *sèche* [SESH].)

- The French for **wide** is **large.**   (LARJ)
  Imagine a **large,** wide hole.

- The French for **narrow** is **étroit.**   (AYTRWA)
  Imagine **it were** a narrow opening.

- The French for **short** is **court.**   (KOOR)
  Imagine trying to **cure** a short man of his cold.

- The French for **stupid** is **stupide.**   (STooPEED)
  Imagine someone **stupid** jumping from the
  Eiffel Tower.

- What is the English for **stupide**? _____
  (STooPEED)

- What is the English for **court**? (KOOR) _____

- What is the English for **étroit**? (AYTRWA) _____

- What is the English for **large**? (LARJ) _____

- What is the English for **sec**? (SEK) _____

- What is the English for **plein**? (PLAHn) _____

- What is the English for **dur**? (DooR) _____

- What is the English for **propre**? (PROPR) _____

- What is the English for **jeune**? (JeN) _____

← *Look back for the answers*

You can write your answers in

- What is the French for **stupid**? _____

- What is the French for **short**? _____

- What is the French for **narrow**? _____

- What is the French for **wide**? _____

- What is the French for **dry**? _____

- What is the French for **full**? _____

- What is the French for **hard**? _____

- What is the French for **clean**? _____

- What is the French for **young**? _____

← *Look back for the answers*

ELEMENTARY GRAMMAR

The French for *you* is *vous* (VOO). Imagine you *view* something.

In French, a verb such as *eat, see, want*, etc., nearly always has an ending *ez* (pronounced AY) when you use the word *you*.

➜ *So,*

- *I eat*   is *je mange* (MOnJ)

- *You eat* is *vous mangez* (MOnJAY)

- *I see*   is *je vois* (VWA)

- *You see* is *vous voyez* (VWAYAY)

There are some verbs that change slightly in the middle when used with the word *vous*.

➜ *For example,*

- *I want*   is *je veux* (Ve)

- *You want* is *vous voulez* (VOOLAY)

It adds an *ez*, but the *eux* becomes *oul*.

Do not worry about this, however; you will pick it up as we go along.

SOME USEFUL VERBS

☐ **Think of each image in your mind's eye for about ten seconds**

- The French for **I am** is **je suis.** (Je SWEE)
  Imagine **I am** a **Swede.**

- The French for **I see** is **je vois.** (Je VWA)
  Imagine **I see far.**

- The French for **I want** is **je veux.** (Je Ve)
  Imagine **I want** your **fur** for something.

- The French for **I eat** is **je mange.** (Je MOnJ)
  Imagine **I eat** blanc**mange.**

- The French for **I have** is **j'ai.** (JAY)
  Imagine **I have** been **jay**walking.

- The French for **you are** is **vous êtes.** (VOOZ ET)
  Imagine someone saying **who said you are**
  here.

- The French for **you see** is **vous voyez.** (VOO VWA YAY)
  Imagine someone shouting, "**You see** me
  on a **voyage.**"

- The French for **you want** is **vous voulez.** (VOO VOOLAY)
  Imagine **you want** a **woolen** jumper.

- The French for **you have** is **vous avez.** (VOOZ AVAY)
  Imagine **you have** something to give **away.**

- The French for **you eat** is **vous mangez.** (VOO MOnJAY)
  Imagine **you eat** a **mangy** cat.

You can write your answers in

- What is the English for **vous mangez**? _____
  (VOO MOnJAY)

- What is the English for **vous avez**? _____
  (VOOZ AVAY)

- What is the English for **vous voulez**? _____
  (VOO VOOLAY)

- What is the English for **vous voyez**? _____
  (VOO VWA YAY)

- What is the English for **vous êtes**? _____
  (VOOZ ET)

- What is the English for **j'ai**? (JAY) _____

- What is the English for **je mange**? _____
  (Je MOnJ)

- What is the English for **je veux**? (Je Ve) _____

- What is the English for **je vois**? (Je VWA) _____

- What is the English for **je suis**? (Je SWEE) _____

← *Look back for the answers*

☐ *You can write your answers in*

- What is the French for **I am**?   _____

- What is the French for **I see**?   _____

- What is the French for **I want**?   _____

- What is the French for **I eat**?   _____

- What is the French for **I have**?   _____

- What is the French for **you are**?   _____

- What is the French for **you see**?   _____

- What is the French for **you want**?   _____

- What is the French for **you have**?   _____

- What is the French for **you eat**?   _____

← *Look back for the answers*

☐ **Now cover up the answers below and translate the following:**

☐ *(You can write your answers in)*

1. You are the young accountant, and I am the little worker.

2. Are you the clean secretary? No, I am the dirty manager.

3. Do you want a salesman? Yes, I want a salesman.

4. Do you eat the rabbit? Yes, I eat the rabbit.

5. You are very stupid, but the receipt is dry.

_____

_____

_____

_____

_____

_____

_____

☐ *The answers are:*

1. Vous êtes le jeune comptable, et je suis le petit ouvrier.

2. Est-ce que vous êtes la secrétaire propre? Non, je suis le directeur sale.

3. Est-ce que vous voulez un vendeur? Oui, je veux un vendeur.

4. Est-ce que vous mangez le lapin? Oui, je mange le lapin.

5. Vous êtes très stupide, mais le reçu est sec.

Now cover up the answers below and translate the following:

☐ *(You can write your answers in)*

1. Vous ne mangez pas le chou, mais je mange l'huître.

2. Je veux la marchandise, et vous voulez la secrétaire.

3. Je vois l'erreur stupide et vous voyez le contrat sale.

4. Les vacances sont dures.

5. Pourquoi est-ce que vous êtes très stupide?

_____

_____

_____

_____

_____

_____

_____

☐ *The answers are:*

1. You do not eat the cabbage, but I eat the oyster.

2. I want the goods and you want the secretary.

3. I see the stupid mistake and you see the dirty contract.

4. The vacations are hard.

5. Why are you very stupid?

SECTION 8

WORDS IN TRAVELING

☐ **Think of each image in your mind's eye for about ten seconds**

- The French for **passport** is **passeport.**   (PASPOR)
  Imagine your **passport** has a picture of the
  Eiffel Tower on the front.

- The French for **customs** is **douane.**   (DWAN)
  Imagine going through customs counting
  "**D'one,** D'two, D'three."

- The French for **toilet** is **toilettes.**   (TWALET)
  Imagine a **toilet** right at the top of the Eiffel Tower.

- The French for **entrance** in **entrée.**   (OnTRAY)
  Imagine making your entrance **on a tray.**

- The French for **exit** is **sortie.**   (SORTEE)
  Imagine having **sore tee**th after bumping them
  at the exit of a theater.

- The French for **suitcase** is **valise.**   (VALEEZ)
  Imagine suitcases strewn all over the **valleys.**

- The French for **ticket** is **billet.**   (BEE AY)
  Imagine being told "**Beha**ve or you won't get a
  ticket!"

- The French for **currency exchange** is **change.**   (SHOnJ)
  Imagine **changing** your money at the currency exchange.

- The French for **money** is **argent.**   (ARJOn)
  Imagine needing money to go to the **Argent**ine.
  (Note: *Argent* is also the word for *silver.*)

- The French for **pedestrian** is **piéton.**   (PEE AYTOHn)
  Imagine that in France you have to **pay to** be
  a pedestrian.

☐ *You can write your answers in*

- What is the English for **piéton**?   _____
  (PEE AYTOHn)

- What is the English for **argent**? (ARJOn)   _____

- What is the English for **change**? (SHOnJ)   _____

- What is the English for **billet**? (BEE AY)   _____

- What is the English for **valise**? (VALEEZ)   _____

- What is the English for **sortie**? (SORTEE)   _____

- What is the English for **entrée**? (OnTRAY)   _____

- What is the English for **toilettes**?   _____
  (TWALET)

- What is the English for **douane**? (DWAN)   _____

- What is the English for **passeport**?   _____
  (PASPOR)

← *Look back for the answers*

□ **Think of each image in your mind's eye for about ten seconds**

- The gender of **passport** is *masculine*.　　　**le passeport**
  Imagine a boxer showing his passport with his
  boxing gloves on.

- The gender of **customs** is *feminine*.　　　**la douane**
  Imagine people trying to smuggle perfume
  through the customs.

- The gender of **toilet** is *feminine*.　　　**les toilettes**
  Imagine a toilet where the smell is sweetened
  by perfume.
  (Note: *Toilet* (*toilettes*) is usually plural in French.)

- The gender of **entrance** is *feminine*.　　　**l'entrée**
  Imagine the entrance to your hotel smells
  strongly of perfume.

- The gender of **exit** is *feminine*.　　　**la sortie**
  Imagine the exit to your hotel is also sweetened
  by perfume.

- The gender of **suitcase** is *feminine*.　　　**la valise**
  Imagine your suitcase filled with bottles of perfume.

- The gender of **ticket** is *masculine*.　　　**le billet**
  Imagine buying a ticket to get into the boxing match.

- The gender of **currency exchange** is *masculine*.　　　**le change**
  Imagine you meet a boxer at the currency
  exchange.

- The gender of **money** is *masculine*.　　　**l'argent**
  Imagine you pay a boxer in money for his prize.

- The gender of **pedestrian** is *masculine*.　　　**le piéton**
  Imagine a lot of pedestrian boxers, dressed only
  in shorts, crossing the road.

You can write your answers in

- What is the gender and French for
  pedestrian?   _____

- What is the gender and French for **money**?   _____

- What is the gender and French for
  currency exchange?   _____

- What is the gender and French for **ticket**?   _____

- What is the gender and French for
  suitcase?   _____

- What is the gender and French for **exit**?   _____

- What is the gender and French for
  entrance?   _____

- What is the gender and French for **toilet**?   _____

- What is the gender and French for
  customs?   _____

- What is the gender and French for
  passport?   _____

← *Look back for the answers*

SOME MORE USEFUL WORDS

☐ **Think of each image in your mind's eye for about ten seconds**

- The French for **on** is **sur.** (SooR)
  Imagine sitting **on** a **sewer.**

- The French for **under** is **sous.** (SOO)
  Imagine talking to a girl called **Sue under** a table.

- The French for **with** is **avec.** (AVEK)
  Imagine a German saying: "I **vake** up every morning **with** a headache."

- The French for **in** is **dans.** (DOn)
  Imagine you look **in** despair as **dawn** breaks.

- The French for **to** or **at** is **à.** (A)
  Imagine thinking "**Ah**! **To** and **at** are the same."

☐ *You can write your answers in*

- What is the English for **à**? (A)   _____

- What is the English for **dans**? (DOn)   _____

- What is the English for **avec**? (AVEK)   _____

- What is the English for **sous**? (SOO)   _____

- What is the English for **sur**? (SooR)   _____

← *Look back for the answers*

☐ *You can write your answers in*

- What is the French for **to** or **at**?   _____

- What is the French for **in**?   _____

- What is the French for **with**?   _____

- What is the French for **under**?   _____

- What is the French for **on**?   _____

← *Look back for the answers*

ELEMENTARY GRAMMAR

To use the words *on, under,* etc., is very simple. You usually use them in the same way as in English.

➜ *So,*

- *on the table* is *sur la table*

etc.

☐ **Now cover up the answers below and translate the following:**

☐ *(You can write your answers in)*

1. He is at the entrance or at the exit.

2. The pedestrian is with the father, the daughter, and the son.

3. The money is in the suitcase.

4. The toilets are under the cash register.

5. Is the passport in the toilet?

_____

_____

_____

_____

_____

_____

_____

☐ *The answers are:*

1. Il est à l'entrée ou à la sortie.

2. Le piéton est avec le père, la fille, et le fils.

3. L'argent est dans la valise.

4. Les toilettes sont sous la caisse.

5. Est-ce que le passeport est dans les toilettes?

□ **Now cover up the answers below and translate the following:**

□ *(You can write your answers in)*

1. La douane est dans le jardin.

2. Le passeport est sur la valise et le billet est sur la table.

3. Le change est dans les toilettes.

4. L'argent est avec le billet.

5. Le piéton est à la douane.

_____

_____

_____

_____

_____

_____

_____

□ *The answers are:*

1. The customs are in the garden.
2. The passport is on the suitcase and the ticket is on the table.
3. The currency exchange is in the toilet(s).
4. The money is with the ticket.
5. The pedestrian is at the customs.

SOME MORE TRAVELING WORDS

☐ **Think of each image in your mind's eye for about ten seconds**

- The French for **garage** is **garage.** (GARAJ)
  Imagine a **garage** under the Eiffel Tower.

- The French for **road** is **route.** (ROOT)
  Imagine roads covered in plant **roots.**

- The French for **bridge** is **pont.** (POHn)
  Imagine a huge bridge over a small **pond.**

- The French for **car** is **auto.** (OTOH)
  Imagine your car has **auto**matic gears.

- The French for **boat** is **bateau.** (BATOH)
  Imagine going into **battle** on a boat.

- The French for **oil** is **huile.** (WEEL)
  Imagine your **wheel** splashing through a pool of oil.

- The French for **gasoline** is **essence.** (ESOnS)
  Imagine putting vanilla **essence** in your gasoline.

- The French for **jack** is **cric.** (KREEK)
  Imagine being up the **creek** without a jack when you have a flat tire.

- The French for **tire** is **pneu.** (PNe)
  Imagine needing a **new** tire.

- The French for **wrench** is **clef.** (KLAY)
  Imagine having a **clay** wrench which falls to pieces when you try to use it.
  (Note: *Clef* also means *key.*)

You can write your answers in

- What is the English for **clef**? (KLAY) _____

- What is the English for **pneu**? (PNe) _____

- What is the English for **cric**? (KREEK) _____

- What is the English for **essence**? (ESOnS) _____

- What is the English for **huile**? (WEEL) _____

- What is the English for **bateau**? (BATOH) _____

- What is the English for **auto**? (OTOH) _____

- What is the English for **pont**? (POHn) _____

- What is the English for **route**? (ROOT) _____

- What is the English for **garage**? (GARAJ) _____

← *Look back for the answers*

□ **Think of each image in your mind's eye for about ten seconds**

- The gender of **garage** is *masculine*.   **le garage**
  Imagine boxers fighting in your garage.

- The gender of **road** is *feminine*.   **la route**
  Imagine spraying the road with perfume.

- The gender of **bridge** is *masculine*.   **le pont**
  Imagine boxers fighting on a bridge.

- The gender of **car** is *feminine*.   **l'auto**
  Imagine perfuming your car to make it smell
  nicer.

- The gender of **boat** is *masculine*.   **le bateau**
  Imagine a boat full of boxers.

- The gender of **oil** is *feminine*.   **l'huile**
  Imagine your oil smells of perfume.

- The gender of **gasoline** is *feminine*.   **l'essence**
  Imagine putting perfume rather than gasoline in
  your car.

- The gender of **jack** is *masculine*.   **le cric**
  Imagine a boxer hitting his opponent with a
  jack.

- The gender of **tire** is *masculine*.   **le pneu**
  Imagine a boxer with a tire around his middle.

- The gender of **wrench** is *feminine*.   **la clef**
  Imagine keeping your wrench soaked in a bottle
  of perfume.

☐ *You can write your answers in*

- What is the gender and French for **wrench**? _____

- What is the gender and French for **tire**? _____

- What is the gender and French for **jack**? _____

- What is the gender and French for **gasoline**? _____

- What is the gender and French for **oil**? _____

- What is the gender and French for **boat**? _____

- What is the gender and French for **car**? _____

- What is the gender and French for **bridge**? _____

- What is the gender and French for **road**? _____

- What is the gender and French for **garage**? _____

← *Look back for the answers*

ELEMENTARY GRAMMAR

You will remember that if you want to say:

He does not eat the fish or *He does not want the customs*

you say,

Il ne mange pas le poisson or *Il ne veut pas la douane*

However, to say

He wants the car, not the boat

you simply say *pas* for *not:*

Il veut l'auto, pas le bateau

□ **Now cover up the answers below and translate the following:**

□ *(You can write your answers in)*

1. I see the bridge but not the narrow road.

2. She has the gasoline but not the oil.

3. He does not see the jack.

4. He is not young, but I am not clean.

5. She does not eat the tire.

_____

_____

_____

_____

_____

_____

_____

_____

□ *The answers are:*

1. Je vois le pont mais pas la route étroite.

2. Elle a l'essence mais pas l'huile.

3. Il ne voit pas le cric.

4. Il n'est pas jeune, mais je ne suis pas propre.

5. Elle ne mange pas le pneu.

Now cover up the answers below and translate the following:

☐ *(You can write your answers in)*

1. Je veux le garage mais pas le bateau.

2. Vous ne mangez pas l'huile.

3. Je mange l'oie, mais vous ne mangez pas la chèvre.

4. Il veut l'entrée, mais elle ne veut pas la sortie.

5. Vous voyez le change, et je vois la douane.

_____

_____

_____

_____

_____

_____

_____

_____

☐ *The answers are:*

1. I want the garage but not the boat.
2. You do not eat the oil.
3. I eat the goose, but you do not eat the goat.
4. He wants the entrance, but she does not want the exit.
5. You see the currency exchange, and I see the customs.

DAYS OF THE WEEK

☐ **Think of each image in your mind's eye for about ten seconds**

- The French for **Sunday** is **dimanche.**   (DEEMOnSH)
  Imagine someone **demands** to see you on
  Sundays.

- The French for **Monday** is **lundi.**   (LenDEE)
  Imagine your relatives **land on** you on
  Mondays.

- The French for **Tuesday** is **mardi.**   (MARDEE)
  Imagine **Mardi** Gras, the carnival, always takes
  place on Tuesdays.

- The French for **Wednesday** is **mercredi.**   (MERKReDEE)
  Imagine Wednesday is **market day.**

- The French for **Thursday** is **jeudi.**   (JeDEE)
  Imagine you were sold **shoddy** goods last
  Thursday.

- The French for **Friday** is **vendredi.**   (VOnDReDEE)
  Imagine Friday is the day you go for a little
  wander in town.

- The French for **Saturday** is **samedi.**   (SAMDEE)
  Imagine Saturdays always seem the same to you
  somedays.

☐ *You can write your answers in*

- What is the English for **samedi**? (SAMDEE) _____

- What is the English for **vendredi**? (VOnDReDee) _____

- What is the English for **jeudi**? (JeDEE) _____

- What is the English for **mercredi**? (MERKReDEE) _____

- What is the English for **mardi**? (MARDEE) _____

- What is the English for **lundi**? (LenDEE) _____

- What is the English for **dimanche**? (DEEMOnSH) _____

← *Look back for the answers*

174

☐ *You can write your answers in*

- What is the French for **Saturday**? _____

- What is the French for **Friday**? _____

- What is the French for **Thursday**? _____

- What is the French for **Wednesday**? _____

- What is the French for **Tuesday**? _____

- What is the French for **Monday**? _____

- What is the French for **Sunday**? _____

← *Look back for the answers*

ELEMENTARY GRAMMAR

When you want to say *on Saturday(s),* etc., meaning every Saturday, you put *le (the)* in front of the French word.

➔   *So,*

- *on Saturdays*   is *le samedi*

- *on Saturdays I eat* is *le samedi je mange*

☐ **Now cover up the answers below and translate the following:**

☐ *(You can write your answers in)*

1. On Saturdays I am tired.

2. On Mondays and Tuesdays I eat in a restaurant.

3. On Wednesdays, Thursdays, and Sundays the boys are dirty.

4. On Fridays, the dog wants a drink.

5. On Sundays, I see the toilet.

_____

_____

_____

_____

_____

_____

_____

☐ *The answers are:*

1. Le samedi je suis fatigué.

2. Le lundi et le mardi je mange dans un restaurant.

3. Le mercredi, le jeudi, et le dimanche les garçons sont sales.

4. Le vendredi, le chien veut une boisson.

5. Le dimanche, je vois les toilettes.

☐ **Now cover up the answers below and translate the following:**

☐ *(You can write your answers in)*

1. Le vendredi je suis fatigué, mais le dimanche je suis fâché.

2. Le mardi vous voyez le dîner sur le pont.

3. Le mercredi et le lundi il est à la pièce.

4. Le jeudi vous mangez dans un restaurant, mais le samedi vous mangez à la pièce.

5. Vous voulez les chiens le jeudi.

_____

_____

_____

_____

_____

_____

☐ *The answers are:*

1. On Fridays I am tired, but on Sundays I am angry.

2. On Tuesdays you see the dinner on the bridge.

3. On Wednesdays and on Mondays he is at the room.

4. On Thursdays you eat in a restaurant, but on Saturdays you eat at the room.

5. You want the dogs on Thursdays.

SOME MORE USEFUL VERBS

☐ **Think of each image in your mind's eye for about ten seconds**

- The French for **I speak** is **je parle.**   (Je PARL)
  Imagine heads of state **parley**ing when **I speak.**

- The French for **I go** is **je vais.**   (Je VAY)
  Imagine a German asking, "Which **vay** do **I go**?"

- The French for **I sell** is **je vends.**   (Je VOn)
  Imagine someone asking if **I want** to sell my **van.**

- The French for **I like** is **j'aime.**   (JEM)
  Imagine saying "**I like jam.**"

☐ *You can write your answers in*

- What is the English for **j'aime**? (JEM) _____

- What is the English for **je vends**? (Je VOn) _____

- What is the English for **je vais**? (Je VAY) _____

- What is the English for **je parle**? (Je PARL) _____

← *Look back for the answers*

☐ *You can write your answers in*

- What is the French for **I like**?   _____

- What is the French for **I sell**?   _____

- What is the French for **I go**?   _____

- What is the French for **I speak**?   _____

← *Look back for the answers*

☐ **Now cover up the answers below and translate the following:**

☐ *(You can write your answers in)*

1. I speak to the wife.

2. I go to the suitcase.

3. I sell the tickets on Sundays.

4. I like the girl but not the boy.

5. I want the potatoes and the drinks.

_____

_____

_____

_____

_____

_____

_____

_____

☐ *The answers are:*

1. Je parle à la femme.
2. Je vais à la valise.
3. Je vends les billets le dimanche.
4. J'aime la jeune fille mais pas le garçon.
5. Je veux les pommes de terre et les boissons.

Now cover up the answers below and translate the following:

☐ *(You can write your answers in)*

1. Je parle sur le toit.

2. Je vais à la porte.

3. Je ne vends pas les vaches.

4. J'aime l'auto rouge.

5. Je suis assez rapide.

_____

_____

_____

_____

_____

_____

_____

_____

☐ *The answers are:*

1. I speak on the roof.
2. I go to the door.
3. I do not sell the cows.
4. I like the red car.
5. I am quite quick.

SECTION 9

LEISURE ACTIVITIES

BEACH AND LEISURE WORDS

☐ **Think of each image in your mind's eye for about ten seconds**

- The French for **beach** is **plage.** (PLAJ)
  Imagine a **plaque** on a Normandy beach, to
  commemorate the fighting.

- The French for **sea** is **mer.** (MER)
  Imagine a **mare** and her foal plunging into the
  sea.

- The French for **sun** is **soleil.** (SOLAY)
  Imagine it being very hot in the sun, **so lay**
  down and get a suntan.

- The French for **sand** is **sable.** (SABL)
  Imagine a **sable** skin coat, with sand on it.

- The French for **towel** is **serviette.** (SERVEE ET)
  Imagine a French waiter with a towel over his
  arm shouting, "**Serve Yvette** first."

- The French for **picnic** is **pique-nique.** (PEEK NEEK)
  Imagine taking a **picnic** to the Eiffel Tower.

- The French for **river** is **rivière.** (REEVEE ER)
  Imagine a river flowing down to the **Riviera.**

- The French for **forest** is **forêt.** (FORAY)
  Imagine going on a **foray** into the forest.

- The French for **countryside** is **campagne.** (COnPANYe)
  Imagine going with a **companion** into the
  countryside.

- The French for **mountain** is **montagne.** (MOHnTANYe)
  Imagine the Eiffel Tower on top of a **mountain.**

You can write your answers in

- What is the English for **montagne**? _____
  (MOHnTANYe)

- What is the English for **campagne**? _____
  (COnPANYe)

- What is the English for **forêt**? (FORAY) _____

- What is the English for **rivière**? _____
  (REEVEE ER)

- What is the English for **pique-nique**? _____
  (PEEK NEEK)

- What is the English for **serviette**? _____
  (SERVEE ET)

- What is the English for **sable**? (SABL) _____

- What is the English for **soleil**? (SOLAY) _____

- What is the English for **mer**? (MER) _____

- What is the English for **plage**? (PLAJ) _____

← *Look back for the answers*

☐ Think of each image in your mind's eye for about ten seconds

- The gender of **beach** is *feminine*.   **la plage**
  Imagine spraying a smelly beach with perfume.

- The gender of **sea** is *feminine*.   **la mer**
  Imagine collecting sea water in perfume bottles
  and selling it as perfume.

- The gender of **sun** is *masculine*.   **le soleil**
  Imagine a boxer lying sunbathing in the sun
  with his boxing gloves on.

- The gender of **sand** is *masculine*.   **le sable**
  Imagine a boxer falling onto a ring covered in
  sand.

- The gender of **towel** is *feminine*.   **la serviette**
  Imagine a towel smelling strongly of perfume.

- The gender of **picnic** is *masculine*.   **le pique-nique**
  Imagine boxers sitting around having a picnic.

- The gender of **river** is *feminine*.   **la rivière**
  Imagine a river of fragrant perfume.

- The gender of **forest** is *feminine*.   **la forêt**
  Imagine the perfume of pine needles in a forest.

- The gender of **countryside** is *feminine*.   **la campagne**
  Imagine the smell of the countryside captured in
  a new perfume.

- The gender of **mountain** is *feminine*.   **la montagne**
  Imagine a strong perfume coming off a high
  mountain in the Alps.

☐ *You can write your answers in*

- What is the gender and French for
  mountain?   _____

- What is the gender and French for
  countryside?   _____

- What is the gender and French for **forest**?   _____

- What is the gender and French for **river**?   _____

- What is the gender and French for **picnic**?   _____

- What is the gender and French for **towel**?   _____

- What is the gender and French for **sand**?   _____

- What is the gender and French for **sun**?   _____

- What is the gender and French for **sea**?   _____

- What is the gender and French for **beach**?   _____

← *Look back for the answers*

MORE LEISURE WORDS

☐ **Think of each image in your mind's eye for about ten seconds**

- The French for **book** is **livre.**   (LEEVR)
  Imagine putting a piece of **liver** on a book.

- The French for **letter** is **lettre.**   (LETR)
  Imagine mailing a **letter** from the Eiffel Tower.

- The French for **postage stamp** is **timbre.**   (TAHnBR)
  Imagine a piece of **timber** all covered in
  postage stamps.

- The French for **newspaper** is **journal.**   (JOORNAL)
  Imagine putting your newspaper inside a heavy-
  bound **journal.**

- The French for **camera** is **appareil.**   (APARAY)
  Imagine your camera involves using elaborate
  apparatus to take pictures.

- The French for **camera film** is **pellicule.**   (PELEEKooL)
  Imagine using film wrapped round your
  stomach to keep your **belly cool.**

- The French for **theater** is **théâtre.**   (TAYATR)
  Imagine having **tea at** the theater.

- The French for **cinema** is **cinéma.**   (SEENAYMA)
  Imagine a **cinema** under the Eiffel Tower.

- The French for **(a) walk** is **promenade.**   (PROMNAD)
  Imagine going for a walk along a seaside
  promenade.

- The French for **pen** is **stylo.**   (STEELOH)
  Imagine a pen made from stainless **steel, oh!**

- What is the English for **stylo**? (STEELOH) _____

- What is the English for **promenade**? _____
  (PROMNAD)

- What is the English for **cinéma**? _____
  (SEENAYMA)

- What is the English for **théâtre**? (TAYATR) _____

- What is the English for **pellicule**? _____
  (PELEEKooL)

- What is the English for **appareil**? _____
  (APARAY)

- What is the English for **journal**? _____
  (JOORNAL)

- What is the English for **timbre**? (TAHnBR) _____

- What is the English for **lettre**? (LETR) _____

- What is the English for **livre**? (LEEVR) _____

← *Look back for the answers*

☐ Think of each image in your mind's eye for about ten seconds

- The gender of **book** is *masculine*.   **le livre**
  Imagine a boxer reading a book before a fight.

- The gender of **letter** is *feminine*.   **la lettre**
  Imagine a perfumed letter from a lady friend.

- The gender of **postage stamp** is *masculine*.   **le timbre**
  Imagine a boxer covered in postage stamps.

- The gender of **newspaper** is *masculine*.   **le journal**
  Imagine a boxer reading a newspaper before a fight.

- The gender of **camera** is *masculine*.   **l'appareil**
  Imagine photographers photographing boxers during a fight.

- The gender of **camera film** is *feminine*.   **la pellicule**
  Imagine developing film by dipping it in perfume.

- The gender of **theater** is *masculine*.   **le théâtre**
  Imagine watching a boxing match in a theater.

- The gender of **cinema** is *masculine*.   **le cinéma**
  Imagine watching a film of a boxing match in the cinema.

- The gender of **walk** is *feminine*.   **la promenade**
  Imagine finding bottles of perfume on your walk.

- The gender of **pen** is *masculine*.   **le stylo**
  Imagine a boxer poking his opponent with a pen.

191

☐ *You can write your answers in*

- What is the gender and French for **pen**? ——————

- What is the gender and French for **walk**? ——————

- What is the gender and French for **cinema**? ——————

- What is the gender and French for **theater**? ——————

- What is the gender and French for **camera film**? ——————

- What is the gender and French for **camera**? ——————

- What is the gender and French for **newspaper**? ——————

- What is the gender and French for **postage stamp**? ——————

- What is the gender and French for **letter**? ——————

- What is the gender and French for **book**? ——————

← *Look back for the answers*

ELEMENTARY GRAMMAR

To make a word like *quickly* from *quick*, or *quietly* from *quiet*, you normally take the feminine form of the word and add *ment* (MOn).

→ *So,*

- *quick*   is *rapide*

and

- *quickly* is *rapidement* (RAPEEDMOn)

- *heavy*   is *lourd*

and

- *heavily* is *lourdement* (LOORDMOn)

☐ **Now cover up the answers below and translate the following:**

☐ *(You can write your answers in)*

1. On Tuesdays I eat the picnic quietly.

2. She wants the red postage stamp quickly.

3. He was stupidly dirty at ten after three.

4. She wants a newspaper quickly at the table.

5. He eats quietly in the room.

_____

_____

_____

_____

_____

_____

_____

☐ *The answers are:*

1. Le mardi je mange le pique-nique tranquillement.

2. Elle veut le timbre rouge rapidement.

3. Il était stupidement sale à trois heures dix.

4. Elle veut un journal rapidement à la table.

5. Il mange tranquillement dans la pièce.

□ **Now cover up the answers below and translate the following:**

□ *(You can write your answers in)*

1. Il mange la vache rapidement.

2. Elle mange les pommes de terre tranquillement.

3. Vous mangez stupidement.

4. Vous voulez la plage rapidement.

5. Je parle tranquillement à la rivière.

_____

_____

_____

_____

_____

_____

_____

_____

□ *The answers are:*

1. He eats the cow quickly.

2. She eats the potatoes quietly.

3. You eat stupidly.

4. You want the beach quickly.

5. I speak quietly to the river.

SOME MORE USEFUL WORDS

☐ **Think of each image in your mind's eye for about ten seconds**

- The French for **house** is **maison.**   (MAYZOHn)
  Imagine a stone **mason** cleaning your house.

- The French for **police** is **police.**   (POLEES)
  Imagine the **police** surrounding the Eiffel Tower.
                                                      (FARMASEE)
- The French for **pharmacy** is **pharmacie.**
  Imagine a pharmacy in the Eiffel Tower.

- The French for **bank** is **banque.**   (BOnK)
  Imagine a **bank** at the top of the Eiffel Tower.

- The French for **hotel** is **hôtel.**   (OTEL)
  Imagine staying at a **hotel** in the Eiffel Tower.

- The French for **inn** is **auberge.**   (OBERJ)
  Imagine someone asking, "What do you do if
  an inn is overcrowded?"—Answer: "**Oh, barge
  inn!**"

- The French for **market** is **marché.**   (MARSHAY)
  Imagine **marching** through a market.

- The French for **bakery** (baker's shop) is   (BOOLOnJeREE)
  boulangerie.
  Imagine that in France, bakeries sell bread and
  underwear for bulls—**bull lingerie.** Sometimes
  the bread is wrapped in bull's lingerie.

- The French for **butcher's shop** is **boucherie.**   (BOOSHeREE)
  Imagine a **butcher's shop** beside the Eiffel
  Tower.

- The French for **station** is **gare.**   (GAR)
  Imagine parking your **car** at the station.

- What is the English for **gare**? (GAR)   _____

- What is the English for **boucherie**?   _____
  (BOOSHeREE)

- What is the English for **boulangerie**?   _____
  (BOOLOnJeREE)

- What is the English for **marché**?   _____
  (MARSHAY)

- What is the English for **auberge**? (OBERJ)   _____

- What is the English for **hôtel**? (OTEL)   _____

- What is the English for **banque**? (BOnK)   _____

- What is the English for **pharmacie**?   _____
  (FARMASEE)

- What is the English for **police**? (POLEES)   _____

- What is the English for **maison**?   _____
  (MAYZOHn)

← *Look back for the answers*

☐ **Think of each image in your mind's eye for about ten seconds**

- The gender of **house** is *feminine*.
  Imagine spraying perfume throughout your
  house to stop a nasty smell.   **la maison**

- The gender of **police** is *feminine*.
  Imagine the police spraying themselves with
  perfume.   **la police**

- The gender of **pharmacy** is *feminine*.
  Imagine buying perfume in a pharmacy.   **la pharmacie**

- The gender of **bank** is *feminine*.
  Imagine trying to lodge a bottle of perfume in
  your bank account.   **la banque**

- The gender of **hotel** is *masculine*.
  Imagine your hotel is full of boxers.   **l'hôtel**

- The gender of **inn** is *feminine*.
  Imagine a strong smell of perfume at the small
  inn you are staying at.   **l'auberge**

- The gender of **market** is *masculine*.
  Imagine boxers milling around a market.   **le marché**

- The gender of **bakery** is *feminine*.
  Imagine a bakery smelling beautifully of
  perfume.   **la boulangerie**

- The gender of **butcher's shop** is *feminine*.
  Imagine a butcher's shop giving bottles of
  perfume free with pieces of meat.   **la boucherie**

- The gender of **station** is *feminine*.
  Imagine bottles of perfume stacked on a station
  platform.   **la gare**

☐ *You can write your answers in*

- What is the gender and French for **station**? _____

- What is the gender and French for **butcher's shop**? _____

- What is the gender and French for **bakery**? _____

- What is the gender and French for **market**? _____

- What is the gender and French for **inn**? _____

- What is the gender and French for **hotel**? _____

- What is the gender and French for **bank**? _____

- What is the gender and French for **pharmacy**? _____

- What is the gender and French for **police**? _____

- What is the gender and French for **house**? _____

← *Look back for the answers*

ELEMENTARY GRAMMAR

In French, words like *my, his,* etc. have two forms: one in the masculine and one in the feminine.

➤ *For example,*

- *the dog* is *mon chien* (MOHn)

- *my table* is *ma table* (MA)

In other words, the *my* is masculine if it goes with a masculine word, but it is feminine if it goes with a feminine word.

➤ *So,*

- *My dog is black* is *Mon chien est noir* (masculine)

- *My table is black* is *Ma table est noire* (feminine)

To remember that *my* is *mon:* Imagine thinking "My, doesn't he *moan!*"

To remember that *my* is *ma:* Imagine thinking "She is my *ma.*"

The same rule is also true for *his:*

The French for *his* is *son* (SOHn). Imagine him singing his *song.*

The French for *his* when it goes with a feminine word is *sa* (SA). Imagine him *si*ghing at a beautiful woman.

➤ *So,*

- *His dog is black* is *Son chien est noir* (masculine)

- *His table is black* is *Sa table est noire* (feminine)

You must remember that *his* is feminine when it is used with a feminine noun. Similarly, the word *her* is masculine when it goes with a masculine noun.

So, the French for *her* is also *son* when it goes with a masculine noun, and *sa* when it goes with a feminine noun.

→   *So,*

- *Her dog is black*   is *Son chien est noir*

- *Her table is black* is *Sa table est noire*

Its is also the same as *his* and *her.*

→   *So,*

- *Its dog is black*   is *Son chien est noir*

- *Its table is black* is *Sa table est noire*

☐ **Now cover up the answers below and translate the following:**

☐ *(You can write your answers in)*

1. My sand is hard and dry.

2. His towel and his picnic were dirty.

3. Her mountain is very pretty, but her cupboard is dry.

4. My forest is green.

5. Her towel is quite short.

_____

_____

_____

_____

_____

_____

_____

☐ *The answers are:*

1. Mon sable est dur et sec.

2. Sa serviette et son pique-nique étaient sales.

3. Sa montagne est très jolie, mais son placard est sec.

4. Ma forêt est verte.

5. Sa serviette est assez courte.

ELEMENTARY GRAMMAR

☐ The French for *your* is *votre* (pronounced VOTR).

Imagine you are a *voter* for your candidate.

☐ The French for *our* is *notre* (pronounced NOTR).

Remember, *Notre* Dame is the church of Our Lady.

This is the same for masculine and feminine words.

☐ **Now cover up the answers below and translate the following:**

☐ *(You can write your answers in)*

1. Your sand is dirty.

2. Our towel is white.

3. Your mountain is heavy.

4. Our picnic is small.

5. My horse is black.

_____

_____

_____

_____

_____

_____

_____

☐ *The answers are:*

1. Votre sable est sale.

2. Notre serviette est blanche.

3. Votre montagne est lourde.

4. Notre pique-nique est petit.

5. Mon cheval est noir.

☐ **Now cover up the answers below and translate the following:**

☐ *(You can write your answers in)*

In the following translations, you can use either *his* or *her* for *son* and *sa*.

1. Mon marché est sur le pont.

2. Ma banque et ma gare sont noires.

3. Son hôtel et son livre sont sales, mais sa lettre et sa mère sont propres.

4. Son stylo et son appareil étaient rouges, mais sa pellicule et sa pièce étaient jaunes.

5. Votre boulangerie et votre boucherie sont pleines, mais notre timbre et notre journal sont blancs.

_____

_____

_____

☐ *The answers are:*

1. My market is on the bridge.

2. My bank and my station are black.

3. His hotel and his book are dirty, but his letter and his mother are clean.

4. Her pen and her camera were red, but her camera film and her room were yellow.

5. Your bakery and your butcher's shop are full, but our stamp and our newspaper are white.

ELEMENTARY GRAMMAR

You have just seen that *my, his, her* are masculine or feminine, depending on the word they go with.

This is very tricky and you will make mistakes.

Another slight complication is that the words for *my,* etc., change if the word they go with is plural.

➡ *So,*

- *my dogs* is *mes chiens* (MAY)

Imagine saying "*May* I see my dogs?"

- *your dogs* is *vos chiens* (VO)

Imagine your *vo*tes are here.

- *his dogs* is *ses chiens* (SAY)
- *her dogs* is *ses chiens*

Imagine saying "*Say,* where are his/her dogs?"

- *our dogs* is *nos chiens* (NO)

Imagine a Scot saying "It's *no* our dogs."

➡ *So,*

- *my*   is *mon, ma* or *mes*
- *his* or *her* is *son, sa* or *ses*
- *your*   is *votre* or *vos*
- *our*   is *notre* or *nos*

➡ *For example,*

- *Our hotels are dirty* is *Nos hôtels sont sales*
- *Your banks are clean* is *Vos banques sont propres*

☐ *(You can write your answers in)*

1. Our pharmacies are full.

2. I eat your chickens.

3. She wants her cars.

4. Our pens are cold and green.

5. His camera films are under the black house.

_____

_____

_____

_____

_____

_____

_____

_____

☐ *The answers are:*

1. Nos pharmacies sont pleines.
2. Je mange vos poules.
3. Elle veut ses autos.
4. Nos stylos sont froids et verts.
5. Ses pellicules sont sous la maison noire.

☐ **Now cover up the answers below and translate the following:**

☐ *(You can write your answers in)*

1. Mes maisons sont sales, et vos gares sont sales, mais ses hôtels ne sont pas sales.

2. Nos serviettes sont sèches et vos timbres sont étroits, mais ses journaux sont durs.

3. Ma campagne est noire, et vos rivières sont sales, mais notre montagne est verte.

4. Votre banque est sale et vos hôtels sont pleins, mais nos auberges sont propres.

5. Nos chiens sont lourds, votre chien est sec, ma chèvre est très tranquille et sa vache est mince.

_____

_____

_____

☐ *The answers are:*

1. My houses are dirty, and your stations are dirty, but his hotels are not dirty.

2. Our towels are dry and your stamps are narrow, but her newspapers are hard.

3. My countryside is black, and your rivers are dirty, but our mountain is green.

4. Your bank is dirty and your hotels are full, but our inns are clean.

5. Our dogs are heavy, your dog is dry, my goat is very quiet and his cow is thin.

SECTION 10

AT THE DOCTOR'S, EMERGENCY WORDS, USEFUL WORDS

AT THE DOCTOR'S

☐ **Think of each image in your mind's eye for about ten seconds**

- The French for **pain** is **douleur.**   (DOOLeR)
  Imagine being given a **dollar** to make your pain
  go away.

- The French for **illness** is **maladie.**   (MALADEE)
  Imagine thinking your friend is looking very
  ill—he has some **malady.**

- The French for **mouth** is **bouche.**   (BOOSH)
  Imagine a **bush** growing out of your mouth.

- The French for **arm** is **bras.**   (BRA)
  Imagine a **bra** strapped around your arm.

- The French for **leg** is **jambe.**   (JOnB)
  Imagine **jam** spread all over your leg.

- The French for **throat** is **gorge.**   (GORJ)
  Imagine you **gorge** a huge meal that sticks in
  your throat.

- The French for **back** is **dos.**   (DOH)
  Imagine making **dough** on your mother's back.

- The French for **hand** is **main.**   (MAHn)
  Imagine a **man** waving his hand.

- The French for **rib** is **côte.**   (KOT)
  Imagine wrapping a rib in a **coat.**

- The French for **tongue** is **langue.**   (LOnG)
  Imagine sticking out a very **long** tongue.

211

□ *You can write your answers in*

- What is the English for **langue**? (LOnG) _____

- What is the English for **côte**? (KOT) _____

- What is the English for **main**? (MAHn) _____

- What is the English for **dos**? (DOH) _____

- What is the English for **gorge**? (GORJ) _____

- What is the English for **jambe**? (JOnB) _____

- What is the English for **bras**? (BRA) _____

- What is the English for **bouche**? (BOOSH) _____

- What is the English for **maladie**? (MALADEE) _____

- What is the English for **douleur**? (DOOLeR) _____

← *Look back for the answers*

□ **Think of each image in your mind's eye for about ten seconds**

- The gender of **pain** is *feminine*.
  Imagine squirting perfume on a painful spot. **la douleur**

- The gender of **illness** is *feminine*.
  Imagine spraying perfume around a room where **la maladie**
  there is illness.

- The gender of **mouth** is *feminine*.
  Imagine spraying your mouth with perfume **la bouche**
  after drinking too much.

- The gender of **arm** is *masculine*.
  Imagine a boxer testing his arm for strength. **le bras**

- The gender of **leg** is *feminine*.
  Imagine a lady spraying her leg with perfume. **la jambe**

- The gender of **throat** is *feminine*.
  Imagine spraying the back of your sore throat **la gorge**
  with perfume.

- The gender of **back** is *masculine*.
  Imagine a boxer lying flat on his back. **le dos**

- The gender of **hand** is *feminine*.
  Imagine washing your hands in perfume. **la main**

- The gender of **rib** is *feminine*.
  Imagine cooking spare ribs in a perfume sauce. **la côte**

- The gender of **tongue** is *feminine*.
  Imagine putting a small bit of perfume on your **la langue**
  tongue to taste it.

You can write your answers in

- What is the gender and French for **tongue**?   _____

- What is the gender and French for **rib**?   _____

- What is the gender and French for **hand**?   _____

- What is the gender and French for **back**?   _____

- What is the gender and French for **throat**?   _____

- What is the gender and French for **leg**?   _____

- What is the gender and French for **arm**?   _____

- What is the gender and French for **mouth**?   _____

- What is the gender and French for **illness**?   _____

- What is the gender and French for **pain**?   _____

← *Look back for the answers*

SOME EMERGENCY AND USEFUL WORDS

☐ **Think of each image in your mind's eye for about ten seconds**

- The French for **danger** is **danger.** (DOnJAY)
  Imagine a notice on the Eiffel Tower: "**Danger, do not lean over.**"

- The French for **blood** is **sang.** (SOn)
  Imagine someone who sang a **song** as blood came out of his mouth.

- The French for **fire!** is **au feu!** (OH Fe)
  Imagine feeling **awful** because you are caught in a fire.

- The French for **ambulance** is **ambulance.** (OnBooLOnS)
  Imagine **ambulances** racing to the Eiffel Tower.

- The French for **help!** is **au secours!** (OH SKOOR)
  Imagine **Oscar** Hammerstein shouting for help.

- The French for **hospital** is **hôpital.** (OPEETAL)
  Imagine the Eiffel Tower converted into a **hospital.**

- The French for **thief** is **voleur.** (VOLeR)
  Imagine shouting "**Follow** that thief."

- The French for **telephone** is **téléphone.** (TAYLAYFON)
  Imagine throwing **telephones** from the top of the Eiffel Tower.

- The French for **doctor** is **médecin.** (MAYDSAHn)
  Imagine a doctor giving you **medicine.**

- The French for **dentist** is **dentiste.** (DOnTEEST)
  Imagine a **dentist** taking your teeth out in the Eiffel Tower.

☐ *You can write your answers in*

- What is the English for **dentiste**? _____
  (DOnTEEST)

- What is the English for **médecin**? _____
  (MAYDSAHn)

- What is the English for **téléphone**? _____
  (TAYLAYFON)

- What is the English for **voleur**? (VOLeR) _____

- What is the English for **hôpital**? _____
  (OPEETAL)

- What is the English for **au secours!**? _____
  (OH SKOOR)

- What is the English for **ambulance**? _____
  (OnBooLOnS)

- What is the English for **au feu**? (OH Fe) _____

- What is the English for **sang**? (SOn) _____

- What is the English for **danger**? (DOnJAY) _____

← *Look back for the answers*

216

☐ **Think of each image in your mind's eye for about ten seconds**

- The gender of **danger** is *masculine*.   **le danger**
  Imagine shouting to a boxer, "Danger, watch
  your head."

- The gender of **blood** is *masculine*.   **le sang**
  Imagine blood coming from a boxer's face.

- The gender of **ambulance** is *feminine*.   **l'ambulance**
  Imagine fumigating an ambulance with
  perfume.

- The gender of **hospital** is *masculine*.   **l'hôpital**
  Imagine carting a boxer off to a hospital.

- The gender of **thief** is *masculine*.   **le voleur**
  Imagine a thief stealing a boxer's clothes while
  he is boxing.

- The gender of **telephone** is *masculine*.   **le téléphone**
  Imagine telephoning a boxer to tell him not to
  fight.

- The gender of **doctor** is *masculine*.   **le médecin**
  Imagine a doctor looking at a boxer after he has
  been knocked out.

- The gender of **dentist** is *masculine*.   **le dentiste**
  Imagine taking a boxer to a dentist after he has
  had his teeth knocked out.

Please note: *Fire!* and *Help!* have no gender.

You can write your answers in

- What is the gender and French for **dentist**?   _____

- What is the gender and French for **doctor**?   _____

- What is the gender and French for
telephone?   _____

- What is the gender and French for **thief**?   _____

- What is the gender and French for
hospital?   _____

- What is the gender and French for
ambulance?   _____

- What is the gender and French for **blood**?   _____

- What is the gender and French for **danger**?   _____

← *Look back for the answers*

ELEMENTARY GRAMMAR

When you want to say things like *the boy's book* in French, you must say *the book of the boy,* and so on.

The word for *of* is *de* (pronounced De). Imagine thinking that this is the book of *de* boy.

To say *of the* you say *de la* if the word following is feminine.

➔ *So,*

- *of the meat* is *de la viande*

- *of the mouth* is *de la bouche*

If the word is masculine, *of the* is *du* (pronounced Doo). Imagine asking "*Do* you have to say *of the?*"

➔ *So,*

- *of the dog* is *du chien*

- *of the arm* is *du bras*

Also, of course:

- *the boy's mouth* is *the mouth of the boy:*
  la bouche du garçon

- *the girl's arm* is *the arm of the girl:*
  le bras de la jeune fille

☐ **Now cover up the answers below and translate the following:**

☐ *(You can write your answers in)*

1. The boy's father is tired.

2. The mother's tongue is narrow, and the father's blood is red.

3. The thief's knife is very big.

4. The doctor's house and the dentist's mouth are very dry.

5. The boy's leg is short but clean.

_____

_____

_____

_____

_____

_____

_____

☐ *The answers are:*

1. Le père du garçon est fatigué.

2. La langue de la mère est étroite, et le sang du père est rouge.

3. Le couteau du voleur est très grand.

4. La maison du médecin et la bouche du dentiste sont très sèches.

5. La jambe du garçon est courte mais propre.

☐ **Now cover up the answers below and translate the following:**

☐ *(You can write your answers in)*

1. Le bras du garçon est bon.

2. La douleur du mari est ici, pas là.

3. La maladie de la soeur n'est pas bonne.

4. La côte de mon frère et la gorge de ma mère sont très étroites.

5. Le dos de votre jeune fille et la main de notre fils étaient assez noirs.

_____

_____

_____

_____

_____

_____

_____

☐ *The answers are:*

1. The boy's (or waiter's) arm is good.

2. The husband's pain is here, not there.

3. The sister's illness is not good.

4. My brother's rib and my mother's throat are very narrow.

5. Your girl's back and our son's hand were quite black.

ANOTHER GROUP OF USEFUL WORDS

☐ **Think of each image in your mind's eye for about ten seconds**

- The French for **left** is **gauche.**　　　　(GOSH)
  Imagine thinking "**Gosh,** I'm left-handed."

- The French for **right** is **droite.**　　　　(DRWAT)
  Imagine you having to **draw it** with your right
  hand.

- The French for **town** is **ville.**　　　　(VEEL)
  Imagine you own a **villa** in the center of town.

- The French for **rain** is **pluie.**　　　　(PLWEE)
  Imagine telling your children to go and **play** in
  the rain.

- The French for **snow** is **neige.**　　　　(NEJ)
  Imagine a horse which **neighs** every time it
  snows.

- The French for **ice** is **glace.**　　　　(GLAS)
  Imagine a sheet of ice looking like a **glac**ier.
  (Note: *Glace* is also the French for *ice cream.*)

☐ *You can write your answers in*

- What is the English for **glace**? (GLAS) _____

- What is the English for **neige**? (NEJ) _____

- What is the English for **pluie**? (PLWEE) _____

- What is the English for **ville**? (VEEL) _____

- What is the English for **droite**? (DRWAT) _____

- What is the English for **gauche**? (GOSH) _____

← *Look back for the answers*

☐ **Think of each image in your mind's eye for about ten seconds**

- The gender of **left** is *feminine*.   **la gauche**
  Imagine spraying perfume to the left.

- The gender of **right** is *feminine*.   **la droite**
  Imagine spraying perfume to the right.

- The gender of **town** is *feminine*.   **la ville**
  Imagine a town that sells nothing but perfume.

- The gender of **rain** is *feminine*.   **la pluie**
  Imagine rain that smells of perfume.

- The gender of **snow** is *feminine*.   **la neige**
  Imagine spraying snow with perfume to make it
  melt.

- The gender of **ice** is *feminine*.   **la glace**
  Imagine trying to make ice by spraying it with
  perfume.

You can write your answers in

- What is the gender and French for **ice**?   _____

- What is the gender and French for **snow**?   _____

- What is the gender and French for **rain**?   _____

- What is the gender and French for **town**?   _____

- What is the gender and French for **right**?   _____

- What is the gender and French for **left**?   _____

← *Look back for the answers*

SOME MORE USEFUL WORDS

☐ **Think of each image in your mind's eye for about ten seconds**

- The French for **slow** is **lent.**   (LOn)
  Imagine being told "Go slow for a **long** time."

- The French for **wet** is **mouillé.**   (MOO YAY)
  Imagine Moses saying to cows "**Moo! Yeh,**
  even in the wet."

- The French for **occupied** is **occupé.**   (OKooPAY)
  Imagine a toilet in the Eiffel Tower being
  occupied.

- The French for **closed** is **fermé.**   (FERMAY)
  Imagine something being closed **for me.**

- The French for **please** is **s'il vous plaît.**   (SEEL VOO PLAY)
  Imagine saying "Please can I have a **silver
  plate.**"

- The French for **thank you** is **merci.**   (MERSEE)
  Imagine thanking someone for showing **mercy.**

☐ *You can write your answers in*

- What is the English for **merci**? (MERSEE) _____

- What is the English for **s'il vous plaît**? _____
  (SEEL VOO PLAY)

- What is the English for **fermé**? (FERMAY) _____

- What is the English for **occupé**? _____
  (OKooPAY)

- What is the English for **mouillé**? _____
  (MOO YAY)

- What is the English for **lent**? (LOn) _____

← *Look back for the answers*

☐ *You can write your answers in*

- What is the French for **thank you**?   _____

- What is the French for **please**?   _____

- What is the French for **closed**?   _____

- What is the French for **occupied**?   _____

- What is the French for **wet**?   _____

- What is the French for **slow**?   _____

← *Look back for the answers*

ELEMENTARY GRAMMAR

When you want to say *of the ambulance,* you say *de l'ambulance.*

In other words, for words that begin with a vowel in French, you always say *De L'* when you mean *of the.*

Finally when the word is plural, such as *of the dogs,* then the word for *of the* is *des* (pronounced DAY), whether it is masculine or feminine.

➡ *So,*

- *of the dogs* is *des chiens*

Please note:

I sell and *I am selling* (*je vends*),
I see and *I am seeing* (*je vois*),
and so on

are translated in the same way, since in French they are the same.

Now cover up the answers below and translate the following:

☐ *(You can write your answers in)*

1. The ambulance's tire is very narrow.

2. The dogs of the town are very dirty.

3. I like the cold rain, and I sell the dry ice.

4. I speak very slowly, and I am going very quickly.

5. I am selling the very white wine.

_____

_____

_____

_____

_____

_____

_____

☐ *The answers are:*

1. Le pneu de l'ambulance est très étroit.

2. Les chiens de la ville sont très sales.

3. J'aime la pluie froide, et je vends la glace sèche.

4. Je parle très lentement, et je vais très rapidement.

5. Je vends le vin très blanc.

☐ **Now cover up the answers below and translate the following:**

☐ *(You can write your answers in)*

1. Au secours! L'argent de la banque est sale. Où est le téléphone, s'il vous plaît?

2. Merci. Je vois la neige blanche mais pas la pluie mouillée.

3. Danger! Au feu! La maison des voleurs est rouge.

4. Les toilettes du père sont occupées.

5. L'essence de l'ambulance est bleue.

_____

_____

_____

_____

_____

_____

☐ *The answers are:*

1. Help! The bank's money is dirty. Where is the telephone, please?

2. Thank you. I see the white snow but not the wet rain.

3. Danger! Fire! The thieves' house is red.

4. The father's toilet(s) is (are) occupied.

5. The ambulance's gasoline is blue.

MONTHS OF THE YEAR

With the possible exceptions of July and August, the months of the year are quite similar in French and English, so images will be given only for July and August.

The French for *July* is *juillet* (pronounced JWEEYAY). Imagine July is *wearying*.

The French for *August* is *août* (pronounced OOT). Imagine the owl begins to *hoot* in August.

The Months of the Year

English	French	Pronounced
January	janvier	JOnVEE AY
February	février	FAYVREE AY
March	mars	MARS
April	avril	AVREEL
May	mai	MAY
June	juin	JWAHn
July	juillet	JWEEYAY
August	août	OOT
September	septembre	SEPTOnBR
October	octobre	OKTOBR
November	novembre	NOVOnBR
December	décembre	DAYSOnBR

If you want to say *in January,* etc., you say *en janvier,* etc.

☐ **Now cover up the answers below and translate the following:**

☐ *(You can write your answers in)*

1. I eat the meat in September but not in October.

2. I was ill in August and I was stupid in July.

3. The blue dog has seven boys in January.

4. I have the pain in March and in April.

5. My mouth was red in December.

_____

_____

_____

_____

_____

_____

_____

_____

☐ *The answers are:*

1. Je mange la viande en septembre mais pas en octobre.

2. J'étais malade en août et j'étais stupide en juillet.

3. Le chien bleu a sept garçons en janvier.

4. J'ai la douleur en mars et en avril.

5. Ma bouche était rouge en décembre.

This is the end of the course. We hope you have enjoyed it! Of course words and grammar will not be remembered forever without review, but if you look at the book from time to time, you will be surprised at how quickly everything comes back.

When you go abroad, do not be too shy to try out what you have learned. Your host will appreciate your making the effort to speak, even if you sometimes make mistakes. And the more you attempt to speak the more you will learn!

GLOSSARY

a (an)	un/une	car	l'auto (f)
accountant	le comptable	carpet	le tapis
am	suis	cash register	la caisse
ambulance	l'ambulance (f)	cat	le chat
and	et	ceiling	le plafond
angry	fâché	chair	la chaise
animal	l'animal (m)	cheese	le fromage
apple	la pomme	check	le chèque
are (you)	êtes	cinema	le cinéma
are (they)	sont	clean	propre
arm	le bras	clock	la pendule
armchair	le fauteuil	closed	fermé
at	à	clothes	les vêtements (m)
back	le dos	coffee	le café
bakery	la boulangerie	cold	froid
bank	la banque	contract	le contrat
beach	la plage	countryside	la campagne
bean	le haricot	cow	la vache
because	parce que	cup	la tasse
bed	le lit	cupboard	le placard
beer	la bière	currency	le change
big	grand	exchange	
bill	l'addition (f)	curtain	le rideau
black	noir	customs	la douane
blood	le sang	cutlery	le couvert
blue	bleu	danger	le danger
boat	le bateau	daughter	la fille
book	le livre	day	le jour
boss	le patron	deep	profond
boy	le garçon	deer	le cerf
bread	le pain	dentist	le dentiste
bridge	le pont	difficult	difficile
brother	le frère	dinner	le dîner
but	mais	dirty	sale
butcher's shop	la boucherie	doctor	le médecin
butter	le beurre	dog	le chien
cabbage	le chou	door	la porte
camera	l'appareil (m)	dress	la robe
camera film	la pellicule	drink	la boisson

236

dry	sec (sèche)	hand	la main
duck	le canard	hard	dur
easy	facile	has	a
eat (I)	mange	hat	le chapeau
eat (they)	mangent	have (I)	ai
eat (you)	mangez	have (they)	ont
eats	mange	have (you)	avez
egg	l'oeuf (m)	he	il
empty	vide	heavy	lourd
engaged	occupé	help!	au secours!
entrance	l'entrée (f)	hen	la poule
exit	la sortie	her	son/sa/ses
expensive	cher	here	ici
factory	l'usine (f)	high	haut
father	le père	his	son/sa/ses
fire!	au feu!	horse	le cheval
firm	la compagnie	hospital	l'hôpital (m)
fish	le poisson	hot	chaud
floor	le plancher	hotel	l'hôtel (m)
flower	la fleur	hour	l'heure (f)
fly	la mouche	house	la maison
food	la nourriture	how	comment
forest	la forêt	husband	le mari
fork	la fourchette	I	je
fruit	le fruit	ice	la glace
full	plein	ice cream	la glace
garage	le garage	illness	la maladie
garden	le jardin	in	dans
garlic	l'ail (m)	inn	l'auberge (f)
gasoline	l'essence (f)	insect	l'insecte (m)
girl	la jeune fille	is	est
glass	le verre	its	son/sa/ses
go (I)	vais	jack	le cric
goat	la chèvre	jacket	la veste
gold(en)	doré	key	la clef
good	bon	kitchen	la cuisine
goose	l'oie (f)	knife	le couteau
grass	l'herbe (f)	left	la gauche
gray	gris	leg	la jambe
green	vert	letter	la lettre
half (of time)	demie	lettuce	la laitue

like (I)	aime	piano	le piano
lobster	le homard	picnic	le pique-nique
lunch	le déjeuner	pink	rose
manager	le directeur	plate	l'assiette (f)
market	le marché	please	s'il vous plaît
meat	la viande	police	la police
menu	la carte	postage stamp	le timbre
midday	midi	potato	la pomme de
midnight	minuit		terre
milk	le lait	pretty	joli
minute	la minute	price	le prix
mistake	l'erreur (f)	prize	le prix
money	l'argent (m)	pullover	le pullover
month	le mois	quarter	(le) quart
morning	le matin	(of time)	
mother	la mère	quick	rapide
mountain	la montagne	quiet	tranquille
mouse	la souris	quite	assez
mouth	la bouche	rabbit	le lapin
mushroom	le champignon	rain	la pluie
my	mon/ma/mes	receipt	le reçu
narrow	étroit	red	rouge
newspaper	le journal	restaurant	le restaurant
night	la nuit	rib	la côte
no	non	right	la droite
not	pas	river	la rivière
of the	du/de la/des	road	la route
office	le bureau	roof	le toit
oil	l'huile (f)	room	la pièce
on	sur	salary	le salaire
or	ou	salesman	le vendeur
orange	orange	sand	le sable
our	notre/nos	sea	la mer
oyster	l'huître	second	la seconde
pain	la douleur	secretary	la secrétaire
passport	le passeport	see (I)	vois
peach	la pêche	see (they)	voient
pear	la poire	see (you)	voyez
pedestrian	le piéton	sees	voit
pen	le stylo	sell (I)	vends
pharmacy	la pharmacie	she	elle

sheep	le mouton	town	la ville
shoe	la chaussure	tree	l'arbre (m)
shop	le magasin	trousers	le pantalon
short	court	trout	la truite
sister	la soeur	ugly	laid
skirt	la jupe	under	sous
slow	lent	underpants	le slip
small	petit	vacation	les vacances (f)
snail	l'escargot (m)	vegetable	le légume
snow	la neige	very	très
sock	la chaussette	waiter	le garçon
son	le fils	waitress	la serveuse
soon	bientôt	walk	la promenade
speak (I)	parle	wall	le mur
spoon	la cuiller	want (I)	veux
staircase	l'escalier (m)	want (they)	veulent
station	la gare	want (you)	voulez
striker	le gréviste	wants	veut
stupid	stupide	wardrobe	l'armoire (f)
suitcase	la valise	was (he, she, it)	était
sun	le soleil		
table	la table	was (I)	étais
tablecloth	la nappe	wasp	la guêpe
telephone	le téléphone	water	l'eau (f)
thank you	merci	week	la semaine
the	le/la/les	were (they)	étaient
theater	le théâtre	wet	mouillé
there	là	what time is it?	quelle heure est-il?
thief	le voleur		
thin	mince	when	quand
throat	la gorge	where	où
ticket	le billet	white	blanc (blanche)
time	le temps	why	pourquoi
tip	le pourboire	wide	large
tire	le pneu	wife	la femme
tired	fatigué	window	la fenêtre
to	à	wine	le vin
toilet	les toilettes	with	avec
tomato	la tomate	woman	la femme
tongue	la langue	worker	l'ouvrier (m)
towel	la serviette	wrench	la clef

year	l'an (m)	**Numbers**	
yellow	jaune	zero	zéro
yes	oui	one	un
you	vous	two	deux
young	jeune	three	trois
your	votre/vos	four	quatre
		five	cinq
Days of the Week		six	six
Monday	lundi	seven	sept
Tuesday	mardi	eight	huit
Wednesday	mercredi	nine	neuf
Thursday	jeudi	ten	dix
Friday	vendredi	eleven	onze
Saturday	samedi	twenty	vingt
Sunday	dimanche	twenty-five	vingt-cinq
		12 midnight	minuit
Months of the Year		12 midday	midi
January	janvier		
February	février		
March	mars		
April	avril		
May	mai		
June	juin		
July	juillet		
August	août		
September	septembre		
October	octobre		
November	novembre		
December	décembre		